IT IS WORTH WHILE

José María Casciaro

It is Worth While

Three years with the Founder of Opus Dei:
1939 – 1942

SCEPTER

London   Princeton
Nairobi   New Delhi

This edition of *It is Worth While* is published:
in England by Scepter (U.K.) Ltd., 21 Hinton Avenue, Hounslow TW4 6AP; e-mail: general@scepter.demon.co.uk;
in the United States by Scepter Publishers Inc., P. O. Box 1270, Princeton, NJ 08542; e-mail: general@scepterpub.org;
in Kenya by Scepter Ltd., P. O. Box 28176, Nairobi; e-mail: focus@users.africaonline.co.ke;
in India by Scepter, P. O. Box 4009, New Delhi 110 017.

This is a translation of *Vale la pena*, Madrid, 1998.
With ecclesiastical approval
ISBN 0 906138 47 7
© Original – José María Casciaro
© Translation – Scepter (U.K.) Ltd., 1999
© This edition – Scepter (U.K.) Ltd., 2000
© Photographs – José María Casciaro & Scriptor, Madrid

All rights reserved. No part of this book may be reproduced, stored in a retrieval system or transmitted, in any form or by any means, electronic, mechanical, photocopying or otherwise, without the prior permission of Scepter (U.K.) Ltd.

Cover photograph: On the roof terrace of Jenner Residence, Madrid (September 1940), with José María Casciaro in the centre (third row from the bottom).

Translated by Helena Scott, London.
Cover design consultant: Michelle Pinto & Associates; typeset by MI Intermedia, and printed in Singapore.

To the unfading memory of
Doña Dolores Albás y Blanc
and
Carmen Escrivá de Balaguer y Albás,
with deep gratitude and lasting filial affection

Contents

Prologue	13

1. Preliminaries (1936–1939)

A hotter summer than usual	19
An apology from my brother Pedro	23
Pedro and the bicycle	24
Arrest of my cousin Manolo	26
The British flag	28
"Will you carry on with the Work?"	31
Letters between Pedro and the Father	34
Parcels to Madrid	35
Playing "Seven and a half"	36
Pedro suggests a plan for me	38
Results of being well-organised	40
A shepherd's adventures	43
Almost alone	45
Spectacular bombardment	47
Air-raid shelter	49
Crossing the Pyrenees: a spectator's view	51
End of the Civil War	56
Pedro in Albacete	59

8 Contents

2. How I met Blessed Josemaría (May 1939)
Arrival at Atocha Station	63
Meeting Blessed Josemaría	65
Lunch at the St Elizabeth Foundation	69
Meeting the Father's mother and sister	73
A walk through Madrid with Santiago Escrivá	76
General impression of the day	79

3. Lights in the post-war months (May–December 1939)
Calatayud: May–June	81
Torrevieja again	83
Greater devotion at Los Hoyos	85
Well-planned summer holidays	87
Jenner Residence opens	91
Studying in Barcelona	94
Decisive encounter with Opus Dei	95
Conversation with Pedro at Torrevieja	97

4. Time to decide (January–July 1940)
Return to Barcelona	101
Alvaro del Portillo and my mother	102
Pedro in Barcelona again	103
I ask the Father to admit me into the Work	105
Report on a football match	109
My brother Pedro	110
The apartment at 62 Balmes Street	111
Quick visit from Chiqui	114
The Father in Barcelona	115
Alone with the Father from Barcelona to Madrid	116
"In Madrid, you are to do whatever you like"	117
In Madrid	119

5. In the heart of the Work (Jenner, Summer 1940)

Jenner Residence	121
People who lived in Jenner	122
People who lived with their families	126
Visitors	128
Blessed Josemaría's friends	130
The Jenner building	131
Activities of Blessed Josemaría	133
Masses in the Oratory	134
In soldier's trousers	136
Fernando Delapuente	138
Offside tally	139
"To the barricades!"	142
My first day of recollection	143

6. Family atmosphere (Jenner, Summer 1940, cont.)

Grandmother and Aunt Carmen	147
"Mother, you're going to spoil him on me"	149
Conversations in Grandmother's room	150
A large and poor family	152
Isidoro Zorzano	154
Walks with "Uncle Isidoro"	156
"Make the whole day into a Mass"	158
"If we're faithful, we'll soon be going abroad"	159
Intensive study	161
Alvaro del Portillo and Juan Jiménez Vargas	163

7. Expansion from Jenner (Autumn 1940)

Train journeys to the provinces	167
Samaniego Residence in Valencia	169

Portraits of my great-grandparents 171
The Martinez Campos Centre 172
14 Diego de León Street 175
Alvaro del Portillo's smile 177
Letters 178
Charity and affection 180
The joy of being with the Founder of Opus Dei 182
"Pepe, you're getting as round as a barrel" 183
Devotion to our Blessed Lady 185

8. Treasured memories (Winter 1940–41)
Beginning of the academic year 1940–41 187
The Father and my studies in Jenner 189
Finishing secondary education 192
Gymnastics and sport 194
Trip for school-leavers 195
Setting up Diego de León 196
Juan Jiménez and the younger members 197
With Grandmother and Aunt Carmen 199
Grandmother's death 200
Grandmother's legacy 204
Aunt Carmen 206
Blessed Josemaría's visits 207
Isidoro Zorzano's hidden sacrifice 208
The Work's first canonical approval 210

9. In full swing (Summer–Autumn 1941)
Being a guide 213
Atocha Station 214
Moments with Blessed Josemaría 214

The María de Molina Centre	216
The first Centre of Studies	217
A fax from Mexico on Pedro's death	219
The Father's care for the Centre of Studies	223
Aspects of life in the Centre of Studies	224
On frequent confession	227
Starting university	228
Teachers in the Arts Faculty	230
The Father and my option for biblical studies	232
An irrelevance	233
Christmas holidays 1941–2	235
Ten-page letter	236
Ignacio de Orbegozo	237

10. University life to the full (January–August 1942)

Jenner again	239
Study circles and visits to "Our Lady's poor"	241
Catechism classes	244
Sports	245
Get-togethers	246
Cultural formation	247
Early friends in the Arts Faculty	249
A curious event	252
Preparing the first priests in Opus Dei	254
Journey to Torrevieja	257

Epilogue 261

Prologue

Some time ago, I read in a book by Henri-Irénée Marrou (a French Catholic thinker well known for his works on philosophy and the theology of history) that nations which forget their past undergo something similar to what happens to people suffering from loss of memory: they soon lose their identity. The act of remembering saints helps to combat this danger. This is because they are a living, vital source of the Church's memory, conserving the identity of the faith. Each in their own way, they bring before our eyes the example of Jesus Christ. By committing to writing, at this stage, some of the episodes I lived through with Blessed Josemaría Escriva de Balaguer, I think that I am helping to record one of the outstanding testimonies of the working of the Holy Spirit in men's souls. The happenings of daily life reflect significant aspects of the personality of the Founder of Opus Dei and the influence he exercised on many men and women.

What moved me to write this book was, first of all, the deep love and gratitude I feel for Blessed Josemaría, which increases as the years go by. I could never sufficiently express in any concise way how much I owe him in this life and, unquestionably, with regard to the life to come. Some of the reasons for this gratitude will appear as I write. But so much will remain unwritten: things which happened in the period covered by this book and in the years afterwards, up until 26 June 1975, when he went to heaven. Everything I can say is little, far too poor, to express my filial gratitude.

I have also been stimulated to write these pages by the admiration and gratitude I feel for the men of Opus Dei whom I met as I took my first steps in their company. Almost all of them have now reached their home in heaven. How much I owe them, too, for their truly exemplary, heroic lives, within such encouraging simplicity and friendliness!

Furthermore, my brother Pedro's book *Dream and your dreams will fall short*, has spurred me on to write down my memories of the first years spent with Blessed Josemaría. I have always found it beneficial to follow the trail my elder brother marked out by his advice and, above all, by his behaviour. Specifically, by following him I made some important decisions: first a daily plan for my work and life of piety; then the fundamental decision on the direction of my whole life, that is, the decision to give myself to God in Opus Dei, to which I felt myself being called with a clear divine vocation; and later on, my assent to a further grace from God: the priesthood. What I am about to do now is much less important: it is merely a question of putting into writing certain experiences which live on despite the passing of the years.

These considerations explain why the following pages were written. I will limit myself to telling what I remember of my first years in Opus Dei, after some brief references to a few things that preceded them. These memories, and subsequent ones of other times spent with Blessed Josemaría which are not covered by this book, have all come to make up a continual, very personal stimulus for me to draw closer to God. They have been like clear directives giving meaning to my life and broadening its horizons. To sum up, I felt it a duty to write these memories down, as my personal witness to some aspects of the holy life of Blessed Josemaría, who was a real giant in the history of the Church; may they serve to help other people on their path towards God.

Obviously, because I was so young and inexperienced at the time, I only skimmed the surface of the Founder of Opus Dei's deep, intense life and of some of the aspects of the development of the Work of God in those years. But this statement needs clarifying. What I saw as a boy, from close at hand, in Blessed Josemaría's behaviour, was sufficiently clear and arresting to elicit a response from within me. Not only did I agree joyfully with what I saw but also, and this is what matters, I responded by committing myself to an enterprise that shone out as being supernatural and divine, for whose sake it was worth giving my life, which at that time was all before me.

As time went on, I necessarily reflected on all the events I lived through then. I have come to understand them with the increased maturity that comes from age and theological training. But the clarity of the summons and the demands of a consistently Christian life, under the invisible action of God's grace in the soul, are not essentially different now from what they were then. These old memories have often been evoked by day-to-day events. For more than half a century, I have always maintained the conviction that everything I heard in those years of my youth was true and that following the Founder of Opus Dei, through an undeserved grace from God, was the most transcendental decision I ever made. Be that as it may, my present aim is to put those old episodes into writing without losing their spontaneity. I shall try to relate simply what I saw, omitting as far as possible all reflection about the facts, except for necessary explanations.

What I will relate covers the period from May 1939, when I first met Blessed Josemaría, to August 1942. By way of introduction, I also include a few other episodes starting from the time I spent with my brother Pedro during the summer of 1936, at the beginning of the Spanish Civil War.

Why do I stop at August 1942? For three reasons. The second is so as not to tire the reader. The first, and most important, is that those were years when I was very often in Blessed Josemaría's company; and the third is that the growth in the number of members and the expansion of the Work to a large part of the world in the years after 1942 meant that I was then an eyewitness to only a little corner of Opus Dei, which was already becoming a big family. Other men and women will be able to offer more direct and substantial testimonies than mine about the life of the Founder of the Work from that year onwards.

Unlike my other books and works, this one is not based on bibliographies and documentation. I have dipped into my own memories of events which I actually witnessed. Only after writing them down did I verify some of the facts, to make sure that the details I had quoted from memory concerning dates and individuals were correct, and to avoid any risk of inaccuracy or confusion. In the first draft I did not offer any footnotes, but some friends who read it advised me to give more detailed information about certain people and places I mentioned in passing, so that readers could learn a little more about them. I have sometimes added this information within the text of the book, but more often I have chosen to give it as a footnote so as not to interrupt the thread of the story.

When I was beginning to write these reminiscences, my brother Pedro was still alive, though already seriously ill. He died a holy death on 23 March 1995 (which was actually the first anniversary of the death of Bishop Alvaro del Portillo). When going through the book a second time I amplified some of the things I said about him, since, now that he is in heaven, there is no longer any risk of my wounding him in his humility. Five days after Pedro's death, in a letter to Bishop Javier Echevarría, the Prelate of Opus Dei, I wrote the following paragraph which reaffirms it all: "Father, you know how much Pedro has meant to me. With his lifelong example, his words, and, to an extent no one can know, his prayer and sacrifices, he drew me gently and convincingly towards the Work. He did it perfectly. In a great measure it is to him I owe my vocation and happiness. I have always been very grateful to him and have held him in deep love and respect." For this very reason I have added some extra references to my brother.

I trust that Blessed Josemaría, from heaven, will be as understanding as always about my observations concerning all that I saw as a boy between 1939 and 1942, which I am now writing down.

If this book does not have even more faults, it is the result of some very pertinent suggestions from some of my colleagues. Among them I would like to mention José Antonio Vidal-Quadras, lecturer in the Faculty of Information Sciences at the University of Navarre. He was patient enough to read the whole of the first draft and offer numerous corrections to my style and clarity of exposition. To him and all the others I am deeply grateful.

Chapter One

Preliminaries
(1936-1939)

A hotter summer than usual

Torrevieja, 13 July 1936. The last census I have seen, taken a few years ago, gives Torrevieja, the southernmost town on the Alicante coast, 18,500 inhabitants, though in July and August the number rises to 350,000 with a peaceful invasion by Germans, Swedes, Swiss, British, people from Madrid, Murcia, and so on, together with travelling vendors from North Africa. But in 1936 the census figure must have been around 6,000 plus perhaps another thousand over the summer holidays.

From Torrevieja a little gang of us, made up of cousins and friends, set off on that 13 July for a hike northwards along the coast, towards the sand dunes and pinewoods of the Guardamar beaches. There were about eight children in the group, all around twelve years old, and a donkey belonging to my cousin Julio Ballester Casciaro. The donkey was almost one of the gang, and we never had to worry about him; he would walk along behind us without having to be led, and I think he rather enjoyed being with us. He carried our snacks and other belongings in a saddle-bag, and when we stopped to eat he would keep close by us: he had a passion for orange-peel and the skins of any other kind of fruit too. He even defended us against dogs on occasion – they would retreat with their tails between their legs when he suddenly turned on them and gave them back brays for their barks.

We walked about five miles from Los Hoyos, my paternal grandparents' estate, from where we had started off. It was a wonderful day: we walked a long way along beaches and over rocks, took several dips in the calm Mediterranean, and relaxed as we contemplated the waves. Night was falling by the time we began our journey back to Torrevieja. The sun had shone down all day, and in spite of having taken water and drinks with us, we were quite thirsty. We went to a traditional-looking café for some refreshment, near the Casino and opposite the fishermen's wharf. The people in the café were looking unusually grave, we thought.

I remember asking a middle-aged man if something had happened. Astonished, he answered, "Haven't you heard?"

"No. We've been out all day, walking along the coast," I replied.

"Here, read that!"

And he handed me the special edition of a newspaper. In large print, it said something like: "Early this morning José Calvo Sotelo was taken from his home and shot dead by a patrol of the National Republican Guard" (this group was commonly known as the "Assault Guards"[1]).

Perhaps it is unnecessary to explain that Calvo Sotelo was the leader of the Parliamentary Opposition to the Government of the Second Spanish Republic. Even at the age of twelve I could grasp the seriousness of the event, and I was horrified. I talked it over with the others and we decided to get home as fast as possible.

In the following days the atmosphere got very tense. Everywhere people were talking about the extreme seriousness of the situation. Young men in red shirts were to be seen around, far more than before: they belonged to the Socialist Youth. Others wore blue shirts, and to begin with I thought they were Falangists, except that there were so many of them; I was told that the young men belonging to the Falange wore very similar shirts to the Communists, at least in Torrevieja, so that it wasn't easy to tell them apart, but people generally knew them and knew which side they belonged to.

Despite all this, with the naïvete of the very young, my cousin Julio and I decided to accept an invitation we had received a few days earlier from our aunt and uncle, Conchita Casciaro and Juan de Dios

---

[1] It was created at the beginning of the Second Spanish Republic to maintain public order in towns, while the Civil Guard saw to the countryside and villages. Its role was similar to that of the National Police now.

García, who was a doctor in Orihuela. They wanted us to go and spend the festival with them and their children, Conchita, Juan de Dios, and Tomás, the youngest members of our gang. So all five of us went off to Orihuela, which was about twenty miles from Torrevieja, away from the coast, on the banks of the River Segura. But soon after the start of the festival came the uprising of the 18th of July. Everything was thrown into confusion. I remember that the cook's fiancé, who used to come and spend his afternoons with her, turned up in military uniform: blue fatigues, a belt, and a large pistol. We weren't frightened by this apparel, having seen it often before, but we were intensely curious.

There were family consultations by telephone, and Julio and I were told to go straight back to our grandparents at Los Hoyos. My parents were still in Albacete, in all the heat of La Mancha, because my father still had plenty of things to finish off before he could take a holiday. Besides being Professor of Geography and History at the National Institute of Education, for the last two years he had been Vice-Principal of that same institute, Principal of the Technical School, Deputy Mayor, and was on the governing council of the Republican Left, Manuel Azaña's party. For some days we had no news from them. The news we got of Albacete in the newspapers was very confusing. I should clarify that my brother Pedro and I had arrived in Torrevieja on about 4 July.

An apology from my brother Pedro

We were back again at Los Hoyos, after the Orihuela festival had been cut short, towards the end of July 1936. Family conversations centred exclusively on the explosion of the conflict: wild conjectures, each contradicting the other, were put forward on the basis of the contradictory news that reached us, mainly by radio, about the two camps the country was splitting into, but also through Casilda, my grandparents' cook, when she came back early in the day with her shopping from the market. My aunts were particularly impatient for Casilda to get back, because she had a rare capacity for finding out everything that was happening in the town: so that first thing in the morning an impromptu meeting would be held in the kitchen among the women. The news soon spread throughout the house, and then began the comments.

In one conversation after lunch, to vary the theme momentarily, someone asked about our interrupted stay in Orihuela. I said something in rather boastful tones about an episode which was itself somewhat unedifying. My brother Pedro told me off, which wounded my pride, and I answered him back. There was a moment of tension, but we both soon gave way, and at the same time everyone else helped to change the conversation. One or two hours later, Pedro called me into his room. To my astonishment, he apologised to me. It was not for having told me off, but for doing it in public and rather inconsiderately. Pedro was eight and a half years older than me – and still is, since I have never managed to shorten the gap – and at that stage in our lives it was a very considerable difference.

That conversation between the two of us made such a deep impression on me that from then onwards our relationship improved a lot. As a matter of fact it had always been excellent. But I found it really striking that someone so much older than myself should apologise to me, so humbly and frankly. From that moment onwards I thought of Pedro as perhaps my most loyal friend.

Pedro and the bicycle

In Torrevieja things were not going by any means as badly as in some other places where the side of the Republican Government had won an early victory. There had been no uprising. There was no military garrison, only a barracks of the Civil Guard and another of the police. Both these bodies, which carried guns, were obeying their commanding officers' orders and fulfilling their proper functions. Nor had the parties opposed to the Government organised any militias, with the possible exception of the few young Falangists. There were only, in being or in preparation, militias of some parties and trades unions allied with the Popular Front. The Popular Front had been set up as a coalition of all the left-wing political parties which had successfully formed an alliance to win the general elections in February 1936.

For the rest, the inhabitants of Torrevieja, whatever their political leanings, were a peaceable lot. People had to come in from elsewhere, particularly from Elche, whose militias rapidly came to be feared, to stir them up to violence against the fascists (*los fasciosos* or, in the local accent, *fassiosos*), as people of the other camp were beginning to be called. Even then there was no bloodshed.

However, there soon began to be arrests, and outrages perpetrated against people who were supposedly opposed to the Government and the parties of the Popular Front. Their property was looted. One of the doctors in the town, Don Tomás, was shot dead by a roving militia group who had forced the inhabitants to give them the names of the enemies of the cause. From 25 July the parish priest of Torrevieja, whose life had been threatened, had to go into hiding and could no longer celebrate Mass in the town. Months before, following the Popular Front victory in February, the parish church and another small church known as "The Shrine" had been burnt down. Nothing was left of either of them but the walls. Even the parish register had been burnt. From then on religious services had been held in other buildings.

Pedro learnt that the priest of the neighbouring town, Torrelamata, was still celebrating Mass. Having obtained a safe-conduct pass to get through the militia checks, he began to cycle there every day. My grandparents, aunts, and uncles were worried by this, fearing that the militias might hear about it and do him some harm. But my brother, who, like all members of Opus Dei, included Mass in his daily plan, persevered in making these journeys despite the dangers. For my part, I was happy to have such a brave brother. The distance was about four miles, but the road went up a small hill, which, in the hot days at the end of July and beginning of August, made the journey harder. In those days only racing bicycles and a limited number of others had any gears. Of course, none of ours did. What is more, in my family there had always been two factions with regard to cycling: my father and I were almost fanatical about the sport, while my mother and Pedro rather disliked it. All this underlined, in my eyes, the merit of those journeys of his, which he kept up until one day he got to Torrelamata to find that the town's Revolutionary Committee, pressured by meddlers from outside, had strictly forbidden the priest to hold any further religious services under pain of serious consequences. That was the very mildest step that could have been taken in those times.

Arrest of my cousin Manolo

The concern felt in the extended family gathered at Los Hoyos under the quasi-tribal authority of my paternal grandparents intensified to fever-pitch when my cousin Manolo Payá Parodi was arrested by a militia group. He was seventeen and my grandmother's great-nephew. He was arrested on the estate itself. Nothing and nobody could have prevented it.

They took him away to Alicante for trial at one of the People's Tribunals which had rapidly sprung up in the Republican zone. He was accused of belonging to the Falange and therefore being an enemy to the cause. Pedro went to Alicante to see what could be done.

Some of those tribunals aimed to give the impression of a certain degree of legality. The one which was trying Manolo appointed a counsel for the defence. Pedro was able to contact him to arrange what the defence was to be. The best option was to underline the fact that Manolo was a muddled young man. He had given signs of being somewhat bohemian in his home town. He was a fairly good singer and well known for serenading girls, so that in Torrevieja they used to call him "Chevalier" after the famous contemporary French singer. So, unknown to him, the defence was prepared along those lines. When Manolo was brought into the courtroom, with his shaven head and rather ragged clothes, the defence counsel based his submission on the argument that the accused was in fact a deranged young man who happened to have signed up with the Falange but might equally well have joined just about anything else... Manolo retorted that he wasn't mad, but his passionate gesticulation merely supplied his counsel with ample supporting evidence.

It paid off: he was only sentenced to imprisonment for twelve years and one day. This sentence was a kind one compared, for example, with that passed on one of his fellow-students, Ramón

Gallud, a nineteen-year-old who was also from Torrevieja. The charge against him was the same as that against Manolo, and he was condemned to death in Alicante and executed straight away.

The family's gratitude to Pedro for his courageous and timely intervention is easily imagined. But my grandfather, Julio Casciaro Boracino, was so saddened by the arrest made in his own house and the further dangers which he could see on their way, that he started to rack his brains to find a solution to the situation.

The British flag

Don Julio was not threatened personally, because his Republican credentials went back a long way. But militia groups came almost every day to commandeer some of his livestock (sheep, goats, pigs, poultry, and so on) and produce, and to take his car to serve the revolution. They used to bring it back a few days later, with inevitable signs of damage, making my grandfather highly uneasy as to the purposes to which they might have put it. What brought matters to a head was the arrest of my cousin Manolo described above.

My grandfather was turning over a happy idea in his mind. His father, the first Pedro Casciaro of the line that I had heard tell of, was of British nationality: his parents were from Naples, but he had been born in Gibraltar, and had studied in London from the age of nine to the age of twenty-one. When his son Julio was born he had had him registered at the British Consulate in Cartagena as a British subject. Although my grandfather, who practised law in Spain, had never paid much attention to this citizenship, he had never renounced it.

Don Julio called together the family council and told them of his plan to re-activate his British citizenship. This met with general approval. Certain official procedures had to be undertaken, and my grandfather said he thought it preferable not to do this in person. At this point, one after another, people began to make excuses. But Pedro offered to see to it. The offer was accepted unanimously and enthusiastically. So off he went to Alicante again, since the British Consulate had moved there from Cartagena some time before. Fortunately, the records kept there agreed exactly with what our grandfather had said. The procedures did not take long. After a very few days the papers were all in order, including our grandfather's British passport and our grandmother's too, since she acquired British nationality by being married to a British subject.

The situation at Los Hoyos changed radically within a few days. The property was surrounded by a boundary wall, built by our forebears at the beginning of the nineteenth century. It was about a mile and a half long and was endowed with a number of watchtowers with loopholes in them. Pedro drew the stripes of the British flag on large pieces of coloured paper and cut them out, and my aunts used these as a pattern to sew pieces of material together for the flag. It was about five metres by three. We had a flagpole made and set up at the highest point in the whole estate, which was a reservoir designed to look like a steep crag, surmounted by a little castle complete with battlements and turrets. Twice a day my cousin Julio – the owner of the donkey – and I would go along almost ceremoniously to hoist and lower the flag. It could be seen for several kilometres in all directions.

The townsfolk of Torrevieja made comments like: "Just look at the cunning old fellow" (they normally used a somewhat stronger term), "Now it turns out he's English!" But the documentation was incontestably correct, it testified to a demonstrable fact, and in those areas along the sea-coast, Britain was held in high and widespread esteem. What was more, everyone knew that the Government of the Spanish Republic was keen to be on good terms with the United Kingdom.

Don Julio grew bolder. He declared that within the walls that surrounded his estate was all British territory. He repeated this with such conviction that it came to be a commonly held opinion in the town. He even used to go for walks around his "British territory" to see that all was as it should be. He would arm himself with a wonderful cowboy-style revolver which had been brought back for him from America by his son-in-law, Anastasio Ballester, the father of my cousin Julio, who was the captain of a merchant ship on the Europe to America route. Sometimes he would be accompanied by Antonio, the watchman. On other occasions he would summon me, providing me with a shot-gun, since I was known to be a good shot, having practised with an airgun which my father had given me years before. The picture of my grandfather, very thin, going along with myself, quite small, reminded me of Don Quixote and Sancho Panza.

Then relations and friends who found themselves in danger began to gather under the protection of the British flag. My grandfather had the little chapel in the grounds fitted out as living quarters. As a precaution, given the anti-clerical fury which had been unleashed, he had its bell-tower taken down. In the main house, several living-rooms were turned into bedrooms and we were moved around.

"Will you carry on with the Work?"

Nearly two months after the outbreak of the Civil War, Pedro received a postcard which filled him with joy and immense relief. It was from Blessed Josemaría. Since the start of the conflict, those few lines were the very first news he had had of the Father or the other members of Opus Dei. My brother had been extremely anxious, wondering every day what might have happened to them. The students' residence at 16 Ferraz Street in Madrid, which had been opened on the initiative of Blessed Josemaría, was the only Centre of Opus Dei which existed at that time;[2] Pedro had lived there during the year 1935-36, when the Work had developed very little, and only in Madrid. The reason for the lack of any news from them was that the Ferraz Street Residence was situated almost exactly opposite the Montaña Barracks. The garrison at this military post had joined in the uprising on 18 July. In response, the Government of the Republic had armed the militias of the political parties of the Popular Front, and the barracks immediately came under assault from infantry and artillery. All the buildings around the barracks were evacuated and then occupied by the militias and other army forces loyal to the Government.

Blessed Josemaría had to leave the residence and make his way through the massed militias. He had put on a mechanic's overall which had been left in the old garage belonging to the house; but he was bareheaded, so that his clerical tonsure, or "crown" as it was popularly known, could be plainly seen. By

---

[2] In October 1934, on the third floor of 50 Ferraz Street, Madrid, Opus Dei had opened its first residence for university students. With the permission of Don Leopoldo Eijo y Garay, Bishop of Madrid, the first Oratory was set up, and he granted the faculty of having Mass celebrated there and the Blessed Sacrament reserved. The residence meant that Opus Dei's apostolic activities – spiritual retreats, circles of religious formation, and student get-togethers – could be held on a regular basis; and it provided Blessed Josemaría with a place where he could give spiritual direction to very many men: young and old, students, workmen, professional men, and so on. At the beginning of July 1936 they moved the residence to No. 16 of the same street. But because the Civil War broke out on 18 July, the new residence never actually opened. Being very close to the front lines, the building was completely destroyed during the conflict.

the grace of God, it went unnoticed. In the two following months Pedro had written repeatedly to Ferraz and had tried to telephone. Obviously, post was neither being delivered or collected at that address, and the telephone was never answered, as the building was unoccupied. Blessed Josemaría had spent those weeks going from one friend's house to another, as they offered him refuge. So he had never received any of Pedro's letters.

Some years later, around 1940, talking over the events following the outbreak of the Civil War, Pedro confided to me that he had even got to the point of believing that the Father and some of the other members of the Work might have been put to death. It remains deeply engraved on my memory how Pedro told me that, during those days in isolation, he made a serious commitment to God to continue with the Work, even if he found himself completely alone. He was twenty-one years old and had joined the Work about eight months before.

Pedro's promise was in line with what Monsignor Alvaro del Portillo said in a letter dated 30 September 1975, the first he had written to his daughters and sons in Opus Dei as their Father, Blessed Josemaría's first successor.[3] In this letter he noted: "At the beginning of 1936, the Father asked me one day, 'If I die, will you carry on with the Work?' Much surprised, I answered 'Yes.' I learnt later that he had put this same question to some of his

---

[3] He had been elected a fortnight before, on the 15th of that month.

other sons. It was during difficult times in Spain, and the Father had good reason to fear for his life, simply because he was a priest. But the only thing he was concerned about was that the Work should continue, that God's will should be done, opening up this divine path for mankind. As for himself, in his great humility, he never considered himself anything except an instrument, 'a clumsy and deaf instrument', as he wrote."

Letters between Pedro and the Father

The immense joy and relief Pedro felt when he received that first postcard from the Father can easily be understood. Further letters followed, all of them short, which Blessed Josemaría signed "Mariano", his fourth baptismal name. My brother says, "The Father encouraged us to be very united to our Lord during those times, not to neglect our prayer or abandon our plan of life. He urged us to plead with our Lord constantly to cut short that terrible time of trial. He advised us always to commend ourselves to the most Blessed Virgin Mary, our safe path, asking her to protect all our lives, our faithfulness, and our perseverance."[4]

After that first card from Blessed Josemaría, letters started to go back and forth between Madrid and Torrevieja, particularly through Isidoro Zorzano,[5]

---

[4] Pedro Casciaro, *Dream and your dreams will fall short*, Scepter, London, 1997, p.103.
[5] Isidoro Zorzano was born in Buenos Aires in 1902. He was the same

who, having Argentinian nationality, enjoyed greater freedom of movement and so was able to be of assistance to various people and to serve as a link with the Father. Isidoro kept Pedro, and several other people both in Madrid and outside, up to date with news of the Founder of the Work and others who were in very dangerous situations.

Parcels to Madrid

For those in the Spanish capital life was full of anxieties and desperately short of provisions. After the Nationalist troops advanced to the outskirts of Madrid, supplies became altogether insufficient. The only roads and railways still open for the transport of foodstuffs were the ones from Valencia and Murcia-Albacete. All the others had been cut off or were too close to the front lines. Even the two routes still open were within range of the Nationalists' artillery, and they shelled them whenever they heard that guns and

---

age as Blessed Josemaría and went to the same secondary school in Logroño. He qualified as an industrial engineer in 1927, and his first job was as an industrial engineer with the Andalusian Railway Company in Málaga. After the Civil War he moved to the Spanish National Railways' Development Office in Madrid. He joined Opus Dei in 1930. "He was exemplary for his hard work, loyalty, and spirit of service towards his fellow-workers, his love for justice in promoting initiatives to help the needy ... He was always a firm point of support for the Founder of Opus Dei. During the years of the Spanish Civil War (1936-1939), in Madrid, he showed his love for the Church and zeal for souls to the point of heroism ... He died with a reputation for holiness on 15 July 1943 ... His cause of canonisation was opened in Madrid in 1948." (From the Bulletin of the Vicepostulation of his Cause of Canonisation)

ammunition were being transported.

When he heard about all this, Pedro, in the first few months which followed, prepared food-parcels on several occasions and sent them by post to Madrid, addressed to Isidoro. Although there was a risk that they would not reach their destination it was worth trying. I sometimes helped him to put them together. He took the opportunity to tell me something about the Founder of the Work and life in Ferraz Residence. For the time being I didn't need any further explanations. What I could see for myself was explanation enough.

Playing "Seven and a half"

As their eldest grandchild and a boy, my grandparents had always kept a single bedroom in their house for Pedro. It was a small but comfortable room, facing north, which made it very pleasant in summer. The only disadvantage was that it was next to the staircase, where an old clock struck the hour, the half-hour, and the quarter-hour with all its might. In fact, perhaps because it was so old, even before striking it always made loud preparatory noises. You had to try and get to sleep in the interval, a feat requiring both skill and practice. For all that, the eldest grandson's own room was held to be a great privilege. But at this time, he had to give it up, and a drawing-room was turned into a bedroom and study for him and myself. A large balcony gave a view of the sea. A desk and some other pieces of furniture were installed. Seeing Pedro's way of life at such close quarters was a real revelation to me.

The people who had gathered under the protection of the British flag spent the whole day talking endlessly. Some of them passed on the news from Radio Seville, where General Queipo de Llano was boosting the morale of those supporters of the uprising who found themselves in the "red zone". Others had received saddening or hair-raising accounts of brutal killings, sometimes of friends and relations in nearby towns and cities. Everyone speculated on the future course of the war. Between one set and the other, people got more and more upset. None of them did a stroke of work. In the evening, after supper, worn out by the psychological strain, they used to unwind by playing a card game known as "Seven and a half". The game would involve a lot of players and would usually go on until after midnight. We younger ones used to enjoy ourselves watching the adults play. Nobody suggested we shouldn't; after all, we were in the middle of a war, and it was the holidays. Perhaps for those same reasons, concerns for our good upbringing and education were relegated to second place.

The only person who went on working normally, holding his own against the disquieting situation, was Pedro. He had come prepared, with a well-organised plan of action: normal practices of Christian piety, study (he was, I think, aiming to finish his Science degree, which he was doing at the same time as his studies at the School of Architecture, in September), and some sport, especially swimming and canoeing which were the kind he liked best. Of course, because of the circumstances, it was not very easy to do much sport.

Everyone else used to say to him, almost reproachfully, "What are you studying so much for, when we don't know what will become of us?"

His reply was usually something like, "For that very reason: because we don't know, I'm going to carry on with my plans."

When he was not there, people spoke about his calmness, and this was something I made a mental note of.

Pedro suggests a plan for me

One of those nights, after watching or, as we younger ones sometimes did, joining in the game of "Seven and a half", I went up to bed. Pedro, as usual, was already in bed, and on this occasion he was lying facing the wall. He had left me a note, which I kept for many years until I lost it one time when I was moving house. It said something like this:

"Do you think that the life you are leading is consistent with being a Christian?

You never pray.

You waste the whole day. You never look at a book. You don't feel any responsibility to repay our parents for their efforts to provide us with a good education.

You don't even get enough sleep, because you go to bed so late.

I can suggest a plan for you, if you like, to put things right. It is as follows:

Say part of the Rosary. I can say it with you sometimes to make it easier to do.

There's a copy of the Gospel here for you, from Grandfather's study" (it was one volume of Abbé Crampon's edition of the Bible, with the text in Latin, a translation into French, and a commentary). "You could read a bit of it every day, say for five minutes, meditating on it and reading some of the notes.

There's also a copy of the *Imitation of Christ* by Kempis: the idea would be for you to read a few points every day and meditate on them for another five minutes.

As for studying, the best thing to do would be to spend some time every day going over the lessons in the French course" (it was a textbook by Ahn), "which you'll find here too, and doing some exercises from it. And for something to read in French, there's another book on the table from Grandfather's study: *Le Génie du Christianisme*, by Chateaubriand.

I can explain some things for you if you like."

I read this note over several times, glancing towards Pedro's bed as I did so. He was still facing the wall. I tried to make out if he was awake. I didn't dare say anything, because he looked asleep. I stood there reading the note: Pedro was absolutely right. I gave in. For all my twelve years and so many months, tears came to my eyes. After thinking it over for a good long while, I got into bed, without making any noise, as usual, so as not to wake him.

We soon talked it over, obviously, and I began to put his plan into action. As he had promised, he also explained a good many more things. One day he told me a lot about the Ferraz Residence in Madrid and the Father (that was what he normally called the Founder of Opus Dei), and about his apostolate with students. A new world was opening up before me. Up till then, I had only known that Pedro had lived in the residence for the previous year. For my part, I took good note of the way he behaved. From time to time I went over in my mind the telling-off he had written me at the end of July.

Results of being well-organised

On 18 July 1936 a section of the population of Albacete, plus the Civil Guard – there was no military garrison there at the time – joined in the uprising and took control of the town without bloodshed. My father was a leading member, perhaps president in Albacete, of Republican Action, Manuel Azaña's party. After the triumph of the Popular Front in February that year, he had been appointed Deputy Mayor. In the aftermath of the uprising he was arrested with other politicians loyal to the Government, and put into prison. But the town was completely cut off and a long way from the other places where the uprising had been successful; it was soon surrounded by a collection of armed forces and militias.

According to what I heard later, an artillery battery with four guns, which the Government had sent for the siege, went over to the rebel forces. However, the Air Force, loyal to the Republican Government, bombed the town and destroyed one of the artillery guns. Shortly afterwards, Marine infantry units from Cartagena and a great mass of militia men managed to enter Albacete and re-take it for the Government. My father and all the other detainees were set free, safe and sound, without having suffered any violence. He told me about it afterwards.

After these adventures my parents, Pedro and Emilia, stayed on in Albacete. On top of my father's ordinary work outlined earlier, my grandfather had given him several other things to do, and in addition the war caused a lot of complications. At Los Hoyos there was a comfortable room waiting for them all year round. As they intended to come as soon as they could, nobody else was using it. But many weeks went by, and they still did not come.

The eventful summer was drawing to an end. Things went on in the same way. My brother had got a job as maths assistant in the laboratory at Las Salinas, Torrevieja. The head of the laboratory, a middle-aged Russian Jew called Chuno Chorower (whose name the people of Torrevieja simplified to Don Juan Chevrolé) and his wife, Doña Rosa, took a great liking to Pedro. Pedro's hours at the laboratory were fairly undemanding, and he was earning his living and obtained documents as a worker: a card for the General Workers' Union, the main trade union at Las Salinas, and the Spanish Workers' Socialist Party card, which he got in exchange for his old Spanish University Federation card.[6]

Above all, Pedro possessed the key to maintaining his serenity in the midst of all the disruptions: a plan for his spiritual life, agreed on with the Father before he left Madrid. This programme included the habitual devotions of a good practising Catholic: times set aside for mental prayer, Holy Mass, spiritual reading, the Holy Rosary, examinations of conscience; and so on. The months he had spent under Blessed Josemaría's spiritual direction during 1935-36 were now bearing fruit in the testing times of the Civil War. Pedro repeatedly called to mind the indications he had received from the Founder of Opus Dei in the preceding months. With the plan of life he had agreed on, he was able to order his life and activity in a way which left the other inhabitants of Los Hoyos far behind. In subsequent years I have reflected on all this and realised from it the worth of good spiritual direction – what Pedro had received, of course, had been altogether outstanding – and a plan of life done well and faithfully. With help like that, a determined Christian can face up even to such difficult circumstances as those of the war.

My brother grew greater in my eyes as the

---

[6] The left-wing Federación Universitaria Española card, dated from the days of his secondary education in Albacete.

weeks went by and I saw the different things he undertook. He looked like someone who always knew what to do at every moment of the day, while the rest of us were at the mercy of whatever news and impressions came our way, and they were often distressing. Nor was I the only one to notice it. It was the general opinion of him, and was often spoken of when he was not there. My grandfather was foremost in admiration of him. From time to time, naturally, Don Julio would ask other people for their opinion before making some decision. He never failed to consult his eldest grandson, and valued his advice very highly.

A shepherd's adventures

The Civil War began to look as if it would last longer than anyone had thought at the outset. They began to mobilize drafts for the army. Pedro had to go and enlist; but he was put into the reserves because of his eyesight, and he soon came back to share the room at Los Hoyos. The same did not happen to other young men who worked on the estate: they were sent to the ranks, and we had to do what we could without them.

Our grandfather distributed jobs. I was put in charge of taking the sheep and goats out to pasture. Don Julio warned me not to let them reach up and browse on the branches of the almond trees, since there was a large number of young almond trees in the area where the animals went to pasture. I got hold of a long stick and a sling, because the goats especially loved the almond trees, and as soon as I was not looking they would get up on their hind legs and pull at the lowest branches. The sling meant that stones got much further than when thrown by hand. There were three very rebellious he-goats. One day, when one of them wouldn't stop snatching at the branches in spite of the stones, I went up and aimed a blow at him with my stick, but he turned and faced me, put his head down and charged. I had to dodge out of his way, hitting him with my rather thin stick. I was afraid that the other two would join him in attacking me, but obviously they didn't have the brains for that. The first one gave in, after several blows delivered with all my strength; I was scared to death, my heart was racing and I was panting for breath.

On another occasion a she-goat gave birth in the field where they were pasturing. I raced to where Antonio the watchman was to ask him what to do. He said I shouldn't do anything, but just let her rest and wait for her. When I got back to her, she had successfully given birth, and there was an addition to the flock. The next time this happened, I knew what to do: wait, and then carry the new-born creature home in a little basket.

I soon gained enough experience to be able to read Chateaubriand or the Abbé Crampon's *Sainte Bible* in the shade of the almond trees while looking after the flock.

Almost alone

Having obtained the necessary papers, Pedro made frequent trips over the next few months to Cartagena, Albacete, Alicante, Valencia (he went to these last two to see José María Hernández de Garnica,[7] who was in prison, and Francisco Botella,[8]

---

[7] José María Hernández de Garnica was twenty-three at the time and had joined Opus Dei in 1935, when he had almost completed his degree in Mining Engineering. He was imprisoned in the Republican zone during the Civil War and experienced all sorts of difficulties and dangers. After the end of the war he completed his Engineering degree and then took a further degree in Natural Sciences in Madrid. Years later he obtained a doctorate in Theology at the Lateran University in Rome. In 1944, he was one of the first three members of Opus Dei to be ordained to the priesthood, together with Alvaro del Portillo and José Luis Múzquiz. He made a generous and really exemplary contribution to the expansion of Opus Dei in France, England, Ireland, Germany, Austria, Switzerland, Belgium, and Holland. He died a holy death in 1972.

[8] Francisco Botella Raduán, Paco to all his friends, was my brother's inseparable companion from 1934 to the end of 1940. We sometimes used to speak of them as "Parallel Lives", as in *Plutarch*. They were both born in 1915 (Paco in Alcoy, Alicante). They studied together for the entrance exams into the School of Architecture, started their Architecture degree at the same time, and both combined it with a Science degree. Pedro asked for admission to the Work on 20 November 1935; Paco three days later. Paco and Pedro crossed the Pyrenees with Blessed Josemaría during the Spanish Civil War and spent several months with him in Burgos. They finished their Science degrees in summer 1939 and began their respective doctoral theses. From the end of 1940 their activities began to diverge and they lived in different places. Paco defended his doctoral thesis with outstanding ability and received the highest award. Two years later he won a competitive examination for the chair in Analytical Geometry and Topology at the University of Barcelona, later moving to Madrid. Paco and Pedro were both ordained to the priesthood in the same ceremony (1946). Paco became President of the Spanish Royal Mathematical

who was living with his parents in Valencia), and to Alcalalí, where Rafael Calvo[9] was living, and other places besides. The head of the Salinas laboratory gave him leave of absence for these journeys without any difficulty.

My cousin Julio, with whom I had hoisted and lowered the famous flag, went to Orihuela to continue his secondary schooling, since the Institute of Education there had opened, possibly at the end of 1936, a few months later than normal. My school in Albacete did not start classes again until 8 March 1937. My cousins from Orihuela, Conchita, Juan de Dios, and Tomás, went back home to continue their studies. My cousin Manolo (who had not really been a member of the gang but sometimes went around with us) was still in San Miguel prison in Alicante.

Society. He combined his teaching and research with an intense priestly ministry. He was Regional Councillor of Opus Dei in Spain soon after Pedro had been. When he retired from his professorship in 1985, he dedicated himself entirely to his priestly ministry, spending most of the day administering the Sacrament of Penance and giving spiritual care to the sick, until he died in Madrid, with a widespread reputation for holiness, in 1987. During the times he lived with Blessed Josemaría he learnt the spirit of Opus Dei directly from him, so that he was able to put it into practice in his daily life and pass it on to others with exemplary faithfulness.

[9] Rafael Calvo Serer campaigned actively during the Franco regime for a return to monarchy and democracy, and, as a result, when a warrant was issued for his arrest he was obliged to leave Spain and live in exile for many years. He was Professor of the Philosophy of History at the University of Madrid, and wrote on history, philosophy, and politics, having a great influence on sectors of Spanish intellectual life. He joined Opus Dei in April 1936 and died in the University Clinic at Pamplona in 1988, surrounded by our care and affection.

My cousins Julio and Julia Casciaro had gone home to Cartagena.

I hardly ever saw my Torrevieja friends because of the circumstances we were living in. The leader of our little gang had been my cousin Carolina Casciaro, who was also the eldest – she was three years older than me. Her father, my uncle Tomás, had died a few years before, and she had now gone to Murcia, since her mother, my aunt Matilde Torregrosa, belonged to a family which was held to be very right-wing in Torrevieja; for example, Ramón Gallud, who had been shot in Alicante, was her nephew. I have kept in contact with Carolina and her husband, Juan Bernal-Quirós, for nearly half a century now, and we get on together and love each other like brothers and sisters. They both helped a great deal with Opus Dei's beginnings in Murcia. Out of the whole of our gang only Adelita, Manolo Payá's sister, was left. She was a delightful girl but was very busy at that time helping her mother to run the house and look after her two small brothers, as well as making frequent trips to Alicante to visit her older brother in prison.

I was practically the only person of my age in Los Hoyos and had to hoist and lower the British flag and do all sorts of other jobs on my own. It was the first time I had spent the winter in Torrevieja instead of Albacete.

Spectacular bombardment

I have forgotten the date when the coastal ports

from Alicante to Cartagena were bombed by night. Perhaps it was in the first months of 1937. At intervals throughout the whole night a small squadron of bombers flew over. The petrol depot at Alicante, which had just been replenished by the arrival of a petrol-tanker, was hit. They opened the sluices to prevent a major catastrophe, but huge quantities of the fuel ended up in the harbour, and all the wooden boats, from small sailing or fishing boats to large vessels, were destroyed in the fire.

From Torrevieja the whole northern sky was a brilliant red; it looked almost apocalyptic. From the highest balconies at Los Hoyos we could see the bombardment of Cartagena. For all its drama, it was a magnificent spectacle. The ships of the Spanish Squadron were mostly moored to the piers around Cartagena because there were no officers left, the crews having tied them to anchors and thrown them into the sea at the start of the uprising. Their anti-aircraft batteries, and those in the forts around the port, opened fire on the Nationalist aeroplanes without hitting any, as it seemed. But the exploding bombs and the flares and tracer-bullets made the whole thing look like an amazing fireworks display. Torrevieja, it should be said, is about half-way between Alicante and Cartagena: thirty miles by road from the former, and about forty from the latter. Every pane of glass at Los Hoyos rattled unceasingly.

Torrevieja had its turn too. We had seen the aeroplanes go over in the middle of a moonlit night and thought that we would not be affected. But one or more of them dropped some bombs on the half-built harbour. A lot of boats were hit. For some hours a rumour went around that troops of the *"fasciosos"* had disembarked near Alicante. The news was very confusing and caused suppressed joy and hope in some, and fear and anguish in others. In the morning the rumour was found to be false: there had only been the bombardment. Positions were reversed: despair in those who had rejoiced and relief in those who had been frightened.

A few days later I had to go into Alicante. The harbour presented a desolate panorama: big ships burnt and sunk, with just part of the hull still showing; countless smaller craft, reduced almost to charcoal, on the sea-bed at the base of the piers; huge quantities of dead fish floating in the water; and the results of the fire all around the petrol depot.

Air-raid shelter

In view of the circumstances my grandfather decided to build an air-raid shelter at Los Hoyos. He made use of some areas that had been levelled out several years earlier, when the system of wells and rain-water collection was enlarged, and a long narrow tunnel was built, which started from the base of one of these areas and went forty feet underground, down to the water-level of a well. The plan was to build a shelter big enough for about twenty-five people next to the tunnel-mouth, with a steeply sloping roof supported on this flat surface and reinforced with lots of sandbags; the whole thing being covered over with earth. Another twenty-five or so people could fit inside the tunnel itself. The shelter and the tunnel between them would hold all the inhabitants of Los Hoyos.

This was a new stage in our lives there. Naturally there were no workmen available to build the shelter. Don Julio directed a team composed of myself, another cousin of mine, a nephew of my grandmother's, plus the mechanic and the guard from time to time, and occasionally one or other of the people who had taken refuge under the protection of the British flag. We were in a hurry to finish, in case there were more air-raids. In these circumstances I stopped fulfilling the little plan of life Pedro had drawn up for me. And this had a prolonged bad effect on me. I grew steadily cooler in the practice of my religion and lost the habit of studying.

I have sometimes thought over these experiences of long ago. The contrast between Pedro and the rest was obvious. The key to it lay in his months in contact with the Founder of Opus Dei, which Pedro had often told me about and, as I realised, in his faithful fulfilment of the daily plan he had made for himself. And I reproached myself for being incapable of doing the same. I had bursts of goodwill and sometimes managed it for a while or even a few days together, but then I would let things slide again. I did struggle on with Ahn's French course and *Le Génie du Christianisme*, by Chateaubriand.

The end of this stage in my life came when I moved to Albacete on 7 March 1937 to take up my schooling again. I was due to begin the third part of my secondary education in accordance with the 1934 Villalobos Plan. Villalobos had been Minister for Public Instruction – as the Department of Education was called then – in one of the governments of the Second Spanish Republic. I belonged to the year which had initiated his Plan.

Crossing the Pyrenees: a spectator's view

In this book my aim is to recount only such episodes as I actually witnessed. Therefore my version of what happened when Blessed Josemaría crossed over the Pyrenees with a few of his sons and some other people, in November and the beginning of December 1937, presupposes that the story of the actual journey has already been told. The reader can find it all vividly narrated in Pedro's book *Dream and your dreams will fall short*.[10]

After various changes Pedro had been mobilised in the auxiliary services in June 1937 and moved from one place to another until he was finally assigned to the cavalry remounts offices of the Republican army in Valencia. From there he wrote regularly to my

---

[10] Pedro Casciaro, *op. cit.*, pp.112-184. What I will relate here is only what I observed as an outsider, meaning what went on in my parents' house in Albacete while the journey was being prepared for and undertaken.

parents. But then his letters stopped coming, in about September or October 1937. Weeks went by, even perhaps a month or more. My parents tried in vain to contact him. First we were worried, and then we began to be really frightened. In my parents' house in Albacete an army major and a captain were billeted, both attached to the auxiliary section. At the time of the uprising I think they had been warrant-officers in the Quartermaster Corps, but they had been promoted rapidly because of the circumstances of the war. They realised that we were worried by the absence of any news. The Major offered his services to obtain news. I remember how one day, when my father was out, he said as much in so many words to my mother, when I was in the room. My mother, with great clear-headedness, made the whole affair seem of small account and very politely declined his offer. Later, she explained to me, "I didn't want the Major to intervene in all this, in case your brother has gone into hiding somewhere; if they looked for him and found him, things would be much worse. If he persists, we'll have to put him off. Things in the Republican zone being as they are, Pedro may have made some decision we don't know about. He may have gone abroad or into hiding. I think if anything had happened to him we would have heard by now. So it's better if neither the military nor the police start making investigations."

After some time without any news, my father made a decision: to go to Valencia to investigate privately. There he was able to contact Paco Botella's parents. Exactly the same thing had happened to them: Paco had also disappeared, at the same time. My father went to the modest boarding-house where Pedro used to lodge. There was very little news, but it all tallied. A few days before he had disappeared, some of Pedro's friends had been to the boarding-house. Pedro had given no explanation, nor had he said he was going away. Obviously, my father did not want to go to the military offices Pedro had been assigned to.

But my father had a very trustworthy friend, a former student of his at the institute in Albacete, who at that time was head of some Government department; I do not now recall which one. He went to see him and explained the case as discreetly as he could. My father's worry was that Pedro might have been arrested for some reason by the SIM (Military Investigation Service), whose proceedings were top secret. Thanks to this man's good offices, my father gained some degree of access to the SIM, enough to ascertain that Pedro had not been arrested and there was no dossier against him; it seemed that there was no information about anything concerning him on the SIM files. My father deduced – very thankfully – that the colonel at the head of Pedro's military office had not so far sent in a report of his disappearance.

He returned from Valencia perplexed and uneasy, even though his greatest worry, the possibility that Pedro had been arrested by the SIM, could now be discounted. Everything else was just guesses, because he had left no traces behind, any more than Paco Botella had. Another possibility was that he had tried to get over into the other zone, but that would have been so difficult and dangerous that my father did not even wish to consider it; perhaps, too, because the idea somehow wounded him in his feelings towards the Republican cause to which he had been faithful for so long.

Anyway, my parents tried to ensure that Pedro's disappearance went unremarked as far as possible, though naturally friends enquired after him. The only person to whom they told the truth was Don Joaquín Sánchez, a close friend of my father's. Don Joaquín was my father's assistant professor at the institute; at that time he was also paymaster for the postal services in the town, and both men were enthusiastic archaeologists. They had carried out a large number of major excavations in different parts of the province on very little money, made a rich contribution to the Albacete Provincial Museum among others, and published several firsthand mathematical works in the Bulletin of the Royal Historical Academy. My father had been appointed correspondent to the Royal Historical Academy some years before, and Don Joaquín was likewise appointed later, when the war was over.

At some time in the course of the next few weeks, shortly after my father's journey to Valencia, a slip of paper arrived bearing the brief type-written message: "Concerning the trouble afflicting you, you can set your minds at rest."

It was postmarked in Barcelona. There could be no doubt that it was from Pedro. This calmed my mother's worries especially, as she had trusted her son's good judgement. My father, nevertheless, continued to be fairly frightened that Pedro, having deserted from the army, might still be found somewhere. Matters stood at this point when, later on, I received a short postcard from a supposed friend of mine, from Andorra. The postcard wished me good luck, and my parents too, and hoped we could see each other again as soon as possible. It was written in French. The handwriting was Pedro's. The hypothesis that he had gone abroad was obviously strengthened.

Months later we got another couple of carefully-worded letters, postmarked in England. These relieved our worries still more. However, my father knew that the Government of the Republic had resolved to take reprisals against the families of people who went over to the enemy zone, or deserted from the army. For this reason he continued to be worried, fearing lest the fact that we had no news of Pedro might become known in political circles in Albacete. He himself, because he had protected many people during the war from detention, judicial trials, and even death, through his activity and his political stance, was no longer considered absolutely trustworthy in official circles, where Republican moderates and minorities were being marginalised by the socialists and particularly by the communists.

For instance, just over a year after the beginning of the war, while the communist Jesús Hernández Tomás, a fellow-townsman of mine, was Minister of Public Instruction, the Government removed from office the Principal of the Albacete Institute, Don José Cortés, who had been appointed long before the Civil War. The professorate thought that my father would be appointed to the post, because he was one of the most long-standing professors, he had an excellent academic record, he was still Vice-Principal of the institute, and because of the political circumstances I mentioned earlier. However, the Government did not choose him, but appointed one of the assistant professors instead, undoubtedly because they considered him more reliable.

Life in my parents' house in Albacete, during 1938 and the beginning of 1939, was permeated by uncertainty as to what had become of Pedro, even though the letters referred to above had reassured us that, at least in the Republican zone, nothing had happened to him. We knew he must be safe and well, though we did not know where. When the war ended we understood his reason for keeping silent about his plans and their accomplishment: it would have been imprudent to do otherwise.

End of the Civil War

After Catalonia, the northern part of the "red zone", had fallen into Nationalist hands, my mother said to me privately, "Look, Pepe. Those people" – this was how she often referred to the Republican Government – "are soon going to lose the war. Help me to persuade your father to get out as soon as possible and go abroad."

This was the start of a sustained attack by my mother. My father put up a resistance, saying, without much conviction, that the defeat of the Government army was not yet assured and that France, which also had a Popular Front in government, was expected to send substantial help. My mother retorted with shattering logic, reviewing the current situation at the various battlefronts in detail, and sweeping away any illusions of help from the French. She wound up, "Nobody believes the Government will win the war, and you don't yourself."

My father offered renewed defence: "But I've helped so many people that they can't accuse me of anything wrong – just the contrary."

My mother's reply was, "Look, Pedro, after a war like this one, and bearing in mind your long years as a leading Republican, we'll have to face the fact that good people are often punished in the place of evil-doers. They may put you in prison, and goodness knows what besides."

Her arguments were devastating. I put in my bit from time to time saying, "Mommy is right," to which my father merely opposed with an authoritarian, "You keep quiet," but without any real force.

My father's next defence was to strike chords of

pathos: "But don't you love me?"

My mother's reply was uncompromising. "I don't even need to answer that. You know perfectly well how much we love you, and that is the very reason why you've got to go, so that we don't lose you for good. If we have to be separated for a while, that's infinitely preferable to being parted for ever."

Day after day she returned to the attack, always when I was there, so that my father would be in a minority.

The long battle was finally won by my mother. At last, on 25 March, my father took the train to the port of Alicante. It left at one or two o'clock at night. It was his birthday: he was just fifty. My mother told me, "Go to the station with him and don't move from the platform until the train is out of sight: your father may be tempted to get off again unless he sees you there."

So I did.

Some days later, the military and political leaders left the town and for a time a power vacuum ensued. But calm prevailed, while certain people went into the town hall and local government offices to take possession of them semi-officially until the Nationalist forces arrived.

There was no violence, nor any untoward event; military personnel, and particularly soldiers of the "red" army, were seen going from place to place, but nobody picked a quarrel with anybody. My parents' house was well placed for taking the pulse of the town: half-way along the road which was Albacete's main artery, running from the railway station to Canalejas Park, going past the Council offices, the Magistrate's court, the town hall and Altozano Square, the nerve-centre of the whole town... The room we called "Mom's Office" gave a strategic view of the main happenings in this road.

Pedro in Albacete

On 30 or 31 March the Nationalist troops entered the town. Huge crowds of townspeople filled the streets to welcome them. A couple of days later Pedro arrived. Our joy was indescribable. He told us the broad outlines of what had happened to him since his disappearance, while we told him all about my father, whose situation he knew absolutely nothing about and had obviously been extremely worried over. Pedro was much relieved to learn that he had taken the train to Alicante, even though we had had no news from him since then. Word was going round that several ships had sailed from the port of Alicante in the days just before the arrival of the Nationalist army, with many political figures on board. We hoped that he had embarked on one of these. But if I remember rightly, it was nearly two months before we received any news of him: then we learnt that he had indeed managed to embark and was safe and sound in Oran. He spent some time there in some buildings which the French authorities had fitted out as accommodation for the refugees. During the summer of 1939, we exchanged letters with him freely. Little by little we learnt more about the circumstances of his exile, including the fact that he had got on the last ship to sail from the port of Alicante before the Nationalist troops reached the city.

Pedro stayed for two or three days, for as long as his military leave allowed. This was enough time for us to plan what we needed to do next, which was to clear the house and put the furniture into storage. My mother was to go and stay with our grandparents in Torrevieja, and I was to go and join Pedro in Calatayud, where he had been posted to the headquarters of the army of the eastern provinces. He also went to see the military governor of the occupied territory and explained who he was, how he had escaped from the "red zone" to the Nationalist zone, his military service, and his family's situation. He must have got on very well with the Governor, who was reassuring in his replies.

A few days after Pedro had left some Falangists turned up, asking for my father. They were curt, but not offensive. However, they took possession of his office and shortly afterwards took away all the furniture in it. But they took nothing else from the house. When we were already in the process of clearing the house, an Italian military health officer was billeted with us. My mother explained the situation without going into too many details, and the officer was very polite about it all.

There were no other visits from any of the new

military or political authorities, except an officer from the section for the recovery of works of art, of the Department for Devastated Regions, who came to take charge of the stored works of art, almost all of them religious pieces, which my father had saved during the war and kept in a large room in the house, permanently locked. Before leaving, my father had asked Don Joaquín Sánchez to look after this. Don Joaquín liaised with the new authorities. The officer was not merely polite but spoke with warmth and gratitude for my father's rescue operation.

In a little over twenty days, we had carefully packed up all the furniture, books, clothes, and everything else. Pedro came back towards the end of April. Our plans were put into action step by step. My mother went to Torrevieja, while Pedro and I set off for Madrid, on our way to Calatayud. During the journey he explained to me some more things about his life after he had disappeared, and about the Father and his apostolate amidst the circumstances of the war.

Chapter Two

How I met Blessed Josemaría
(May 1939)

Arrival at Atocha Station

Madrid, end of April 1939. From Albacete, on our way to Calatayud, my brother Pedro and I stopped off for a few days in the Spanish capital, as we had planned. We made the train journey as best we could, travelling third-class, of course, at least as far as the tickets were concerned; in fact, since there were so many passengers we spent most of the journey in the corridor of the train, unable to move. Most of them were returning home after several years to take up their lives in the city from where they had been forced to flee by the Civil War. They were bringing with them as much as they could: countless packages with goodness knows what inside, bags and baskets of food, small items of furniture, and everything they thought might come in useful to reorganize themselves in their old houses or in other places, if theirs had been destroyed.

I do not remember what time it was when we arrived at Atocha Station, but it was certainly very late at night. There was no time to lose in finding somewhere to stay. Once the train had stopped, we waited a good while in the corridor of the carriage without seeing any perceptible movement of the passengers because their extraordinary, voluminous luggage blocked everything. We then decided to leave the train by the window. We were not the only ones to have recourse to this method, which was used frequently in the weeks after the end of the war. I got out first. Pedro handed me the suitcases, and was preparing to get out in the same way, when some "Assault Guards" proceeded somewhat aggressively to clear people off the tracks. They were right to do so, but they did it in a violent way. One of them, while I was walking across the tracks towards the platform, with suitcases in both hands, came towards me, shouting, and hit me so hard on the back with his truncheon that I couldn't speak for pain. I remember thinking that this guard was a giant, undoubtedly because of my own feeling of inferiority. Then I heard Pedro's voice, yelling a well-chosen expletive – a swear word – at him. He came racing towards us; he was, of course, in soldier's uniform. This was the first time I had ever heard my brother addressing anybody in such terms. The guard apologised, excusing himself on the grounds that the proceedings were highly dangerous and that they had been given strict orders.

We went to the Hotel Mediodía, in Atocha Square, opposite the station, and booked a room for the night, since it was too late to go anywhere else. After that first night, I stayed with my uncle Mariano and aunt Juana, cousins of my mother, in Toledo Street, while Pedro stayed at the rectory of the Royal Foundation of St Elizabeth,[1] where, a month earlier, when the war ended, Blessed Josemaría had once again gone to live, with his family and a few members of the Work, since the Residence at 16 Ferraz Street had been completely destroyed.[2]

Meeting Blessed Josemaría

We had been in Madrid for perhaps two days when Pedro told me that if I wanted to meet the Father I could, because he had told Pedro that he would like to invite me to lunch. As I was then just about sixteen, the invitation was flattering and greatly appreciated. I was surprised to think of someone like the Founder of the Work being as kind as that to me; it seemed almost disproportionate. As a result of what Pedro had told me and what I had seen for myself, especially during the first months of the war in Torre-

---

[1] This institution was an ancient royal foundation, which in those days depended canonically on the diocese of Madrid-Alcalá. Before 1936, Blessed Josemaría had been appointed rector to the Royal Foundation by the bishop, Don Leopoldo Eijo y Garay. It contained two religious communities: a convent of enclosed Augustinian nuns, founded by Blessed Alonso de Orozco in 1589 under the patronage of Philip II; and another of nuns of the Assumption, who ran a girls' school. Both communities shared the use of St Elizabeth's Church, where Blessed Josemaría often celebrated Mass and heard confessions. The Foundation buildings included a rectory. This had been occupied at some stage before the Civil War by the Father, his mother, his sister Carmen, and his brother Santiago. At the end of the war, the Father went to live there again until the residence for university students at 6 Jenner Street opened in July 1939.

[2] See Chapter One, footnote 2.

vieja, I felt very keen indeed to meet him. I had not yet seen any photographs of him, or read anything he had written, so that I had not formed the slightest idea of what he might look like.

I went along with Pedro a little before lunchtime. When we arrived at the Rectory of the Royal Foundation of St. Elizabeth, Pedro, if I remember rightly, took out a key and opened the front door of the flat. This small detail gave me a certain degree of confidence. We went in, he knocked at a door, and we heard someone say, "Come in!" We went through into the room and Pedro tried to introduce me to the Founder of the Work. He didn't have time. He had hardly said, "Father, this is . . ." when the Father got up from where he had been sitting behind a desk, and as I bent to kiss his hand in the customary greeting for a priest, he said to me (and I think these were his exact words), "I have prayed a lot to the Lord for you."

I had not been expecting such a friendly, affectionate reception. I realised quite clearly that this was no mere form of words, but the simple truth. My brother, I thought, must surely have spoken to him about me, but I didn't have time to think any more about his reception. It made such an impression on me that I cannot remember the short conversation that followed. Those first words alone remained engraved on my memory.

What I do remember is what the Father looked like that day: he was very thin; he looked much younger than I had imagined. What was most unexpected was his affectionate behaviour, the way he inspired immediate trust, although we had never met till that moment. That first meeting was a surprise to me, despite the things Pedro had told me.

For the rest, the Father was wearing a very big black skull-cap, which I never saw him wear again. His office was quite small, very modestly furnished in imitation Spanish Renaissance style: a small desk, a bookshelf, one or two little rush-bottomed chairs, and a few other chairs which matched the rest of the furniture, stained a very dark brown.

Up till then I had met very few priests; all of them were excellent men, adorned with many virtues. I had never been on familiar terms with them; the only time I had spoken to them was when I went to confession, and during the three years of the war that was only twice. I respected them, partly because of the atmosphere in my mother's family. But for me they were distant and unknown, like people belonging to another world, with whom I felt no desire to converse. There were no priests or religious either in my mother's or my father's family, at least not that I had met or heard of.

The only priest I had had much to do with, and that in the educational sphere, was Don Antonio Martínez Ortiz, Professor of Latin at the Albacete Institute, for whom I felt a warm liking. From February 1936, after the victory of the Popular Front in the general elections, the situation in the town became dangerous for priests, who were insulted and threatened with violence in the streets. Don Antonio had then begun to wear ordinary clothes when he went out. During the Civil War he continued to work in the Cathedral, thanks to the effective protection afforded by some of his near relations, who were of good standing in left-wing political circles. He was an excellent teacher, and I am indebted to him for having introduced me to Latin sympathetically and enthusiastically. In class and out of it he kept on friendly, cordial terms with his pupils: he was always accessible, attentive, and interested in our concerns (although I had not gone to him for any personal advice) and in our group activities. For example, he was the only teacher who went to the student football matches and commented on our activities. He was perhaps the most popular of the teachers there.

During the war, in Albacete, I had gone to confession to another priest who had taken refuge in the house of some relatives of his; I was impressed by his courage amidst the danger involved in exercising his ministry, however discreetly. But that was the sum total of my contact with priests up till then. I found the Father's personality very different from what I had imagined. In spite of the difference in our ages and situations, and my natural respect for him, I remember that I immediately had a clear feeling of trust and closeness. At the same time I began to discover another dimension of what a priest really is. I think I am right in saying that from that very moment, building on the basis of the things Pedro had told me, new ideas started forming in my mind: the image of the priest, which I had held in respect since I was a child but which had seemed somehow alien, I could now see directly, from close at hand, in the person of the Father.

Obviously, I cannot know what the grace of God was performing in my soul, except though the effects it produced. What is clear is that from those very first moments of meeting Blessed Josemaría, I experienced a new happiness and felt as if I had known him for a very long time after just those few minutes. But it is not only I who felt like that. Other people have said the same thing to me at different times in later years.

Lunch at the St Elizabeth Foundation

A few minutes later we went into a larger, rectangular room. There was a long table in the middle. Although I am not sure, I vaguely remember that it wasn't a real table but two trestles with boards laid on them, covered with a number of table-cloths. At the sides, along the walls, there were four or five soldiers' bed-rolls, rolled up in blankets. In one corner there was a standard lamp and two or three small wooden chairs with white wicker seats. There were already some young men in the room: Santiago,[3] the

---

[3] Santiago Escrivá de Balaguer was born on 28 February 1919; he died on 25 December 1994. He was a lawyer, with an office in Madrid. He helped the Work generously from his childhood up till the time of his death, with constant sacrifice. I remember having heard Blessed Josemaría say more than once that his mother and sister had helped the development of the apostolate very effectively, especially in the years

Father's younger brother, Isidoro Zorzano, and two or three more, also in military uniforms, whose names I do not remember and whose faces have also faded from my memory.

The meal was a lively one. The Father started asking the people there for news of other young men who had taken part in the work of Christian formation given mainly in the DYA Academy[4] and then in the Ferraz Street students' residence. He was very keen to hear about what they were doing and to re-establish contact with them. There were very many

---

when it was just starting, and that his brother Santiago "had suffered for it". Those words remained in my memory because on plenty of occasions I saw for myself the sacrifice and limitations of all kinds involved in his living for several years first in the residence at 6 Jenner Street and then at 14 Diego de León Street, in the same house as all of us, who were mostly very young, and in having to adapt to the timetable of the Centres of the Work, their poverty and the obvious discomfort, and being unable to invite his friends round in the normal way, and so on. I always saw Santiago put up with this sort of limitation gracefully and cheerfully, without the slightest complaint. In time we began to talk about him as "Uncle Santiago", though when speaking to him we always said "Santiago". Having taken his degree he became a competent lawyer, the father of nine children, and an excellent husband. I saw in him an example of a Christian gentleman, hard-working, simple, a good friend, and a man of sincere piety.

[4] DYA officially stood for *Derecho y Arquitectura*, Law and Architecture, but in Blessed Josemaría's mind it really meant *Dios y Audacia*, God and Daring. The Academy coached people studying for degrees in those two subjects, and in it the Father gave spiritual direction to many students, young professional men, and others. He also gave circles and talks on Christian living and preached on spiritual retreats. It was a flat in a building on the corner of Luchana Street and Don Juan de Austria Street, in the Chamberí district. It had opened at the beginning of December 1933 and had functioned until October 1934; it was then transferred to the university hall of residence at 50 Ferraz Street, which offered broader possibilities.

names mentioned, and all sorts of different things had happened to them.

I soon began to understand the motive underlying the Father's questions: it was his affection, his human and supernatural love for all the people he had come into contact with as a priest, contact which had been cut short by the Civil War and the division of Spain into two zones. What had become of each of those people during the three terrible years of the conflict? And, still more, now that the war was over, he felt the urgent need to make up for lost time in fulfilling the sovereign will of God which he had seen so clearly since 2 October 1928: "to do Opus Dei", a phrase he often repeated. The Father knew himself to be an instrument to spread the message of Opus Dei among people of all cultures, making work and all the other circumstances of life into an opportunity for meeting God. His existence had no other aim than to fulfil what God wanted without delay.

The general tone of his life had been unaltered during the years of the Civil War: ceaseless prayer and suffering and severe penance. His apostolic activity, although it never stopped, had been restricted by the obvious difficulties. Now that the conflict was over, it was time to give it a new, vigorous impetus, without abandoning a jot of his prayer and mortification. His zeal for souls and his sense of his responsibility to "obey an imperative command from Christ," to quote another phrase which he had first written many years before, led him to renew contact with people he had known before and to meet new people. Pedro told me something of all this in the couple of days we spent in Madrid and still more during our ensuing journey to Calatayud.

The tone of the conversation in the improvised dining room in the St Elizabeth Foundation was both serious and very jovial. I was a bit like someone watching a game of tennis: looking from one person to another as each person took up the conversation. From time to time the Father would speak to me, undoubtedly so that I should not feel left out among so many people I did not know; he did this out of his extreme courtesy. Although I could not follow the discussion, since I knew nothing about it, the whole session was a very pleasant one. Perhaps it is not easy to explain why, but it was so. We did not linger for very long after the meal. I think the only one who did not have something to do was myself. The rest of them soon went away, and Santiago Escrivá and I were left alone.

Someone asked me recently, "What did you have for lunch that day?" I had to answer, "I can't remember."

"And who waited at table?"

To this I can say with certainty: no one. I was sitting with my back to the door. From time to time I saw one or other of the people get up from the table, go over to the door, and without having left the room return with a dish, which was then passed round the table for each person to help himself. Obviously, it did not occur to me to observe more closely. From what I am about to relate, the solution to the above question can be deduced, reaching the same conclusion as I have since arrived at myself.

Meeting the Father's mother and sister

The Father took me into the kitchen with Santiago. It was quite big, with old-fashioned ovens of the kind that had a sort of grid on top and an oblong opening at one side for adding wood-chips or small coals. In the kitchen were Blessed Josemaría's mother, Doña María Dolores Albás,[5] his sister, Carmen Escrivá,[6] and no one

---

[5] Doña María Dolores Albás y Blanc was born in Barbastro on 23rd March 1877. She married Don José Escrivá y Corzán in 1898. She had two sons and four daughters: Carmen (1899), Josemaría (1902), and then Asuncion (1905), Dolores (1907), and Rosario (1909), and ten years later, Santiago (1919). She was widowed in 1924, when Don José died on 27 November. From then on she devoted all her care to her three surviving children, Carmen, Josemaría, and Santiago. Following Josemaría, who was ordained a priest in 1925, she moved from Logroño to Saragossa and then to Madrid. There, her modest house was the first centre of formation for the members of the Work before the Spanish Civil War. With Carmen and Santiago she moved into the rectory of St Elizabeth's to be with Josemaría, shortly before the outbreak of the Civil War. In July 1939, at Josemaría's request, she and Carmen moved to the students' residence at 6 Jenner Street, where they took charge of the catering. This made an invaluable contribution to creating the atmosphere of warmth and training in Christian virtues, on the model of the Holy Family at Nazareth, in the Centres which are home to some members of the Prelature of Opus Dei, who are more directly in charge of the tasks of formation. In November 1940 she and Carmen moved to do the same work at 14 Diego de León Street, which was to be the first seat of Opus Dei's government. She died there on 22 April 1941, after a short illness at the end of years of cheerful, unobtrusive dedication to the needs of the Work, before the women of Opus Dei were able to take on the task of catering.

else. He introduced me (I don't remember exactly how, though I believe it was basically as Pedro Casciaro's brother), and left. They were still in the middle of washing up after our lunch. As they worked, we joined in a lively, friendly conversation.

It was an odd gathering, composed of Doña María Dolores, who was sixty-two, Carmen, who was forty, Santiago, twenty, and myself, going on for sixteen. Although I had never met any of the other three before, I felt as if I were in my own home. Doña Dolores, Carmen, and Santiago treated me extremely affectionately and shared their family warmth with me. We talked about different things, including, as

---

[6] Carmen Escrivá was Blessed Josemaría's elder sister. She was born in Barbastro in 1899 and died in Rome in 1957. She never married but, with Doña Dolores, dedicated her life to helping her brother Josemaría, particularly after 1932, and so contributed to creating the Christian family atmosphere so characteristic of the lives of the members of Opus Dei, at 6 Jenner Street and afterwards at 14 Diego de León Street. After a short gap at the beginning of the 1950s, when she lived with Santiago in a flat in Madrid, the Father asked her to help again and she moved to Salto di Fondi, Italy (see the following footnote), where she undertook, single-handedly, the work she was by now so expert at. As the Father's sister she soon became "Aunt Carmen" to the members of the Work. She was always prepared to render Opus Dei whatever services God asked of her through Blessed Josemaría, and there were many of them, accomplished by her with silent and heroic sacrifice. Three days after her death on 20 June 1957, the Father could justly say of his sister, who had never asked for admission to the Work, "She has taught us how to live and how to die in Opus Dei: without making any noise, disappearing without anyone noticing apart from ourselves, who were very close to her." On the day she died, during the Mass he celebrated immediately for the repose of his sister's soul, Blessed Josemaría received a grace from God: the certainty that Carmen was already in heaven. He wrote this down and left it in a sealed envelope to be opened after he died; this was done by Monsignor Alvaro del Portillo in 1975.

was usual in those times, the things that had befallen us in the war. They knew about my situation and were very understanding and discreet in referring to it, and even helped me not to worry – because we still did not know for sure what had happened to my father.

I remember Doña Dolores as a simple, elegant person, affectionate but not affected, and very attractive. She had an absolutely clear complexion and not a single wrinkle on her face; her hair, which was already white, in contrast with her otherwise youthful appearance, was gathered into a simple, graceful bun at the back of her head. She looked the same and did her hair in the same way until her death in April 1941. While she joined in the conversation she did not stop working; first, as I said, doing the washing-up with Carmen; then they both started mending clothes. I also remember Carmen that day. Like her mother's, her contribution to the conversation was simple, elegant, friendly, and cheerful. Santiago was slightly quieter, but also took part.

At about five o'clock in the afternoon Blessed Josemaría came back into the kitchen. He asked Santiago whether he thought it was long enough since lunchtime to be thinking about having tea. Santiago said yes, and then he asked me; I agreed with Santiago. Then Doña Dolores and Carmen made us a tempting snack. I do remember what this was: ham sandwiches and white coffee. After the shortages of the war, it seemed extra-glorious to us by contrast. The Father went out straight away. Doña Dolores and

Carmen, still sewing, kept up the lively conversation. But only for a short time. The Father came back and asked Santiago if he had time to show me round Madrid a little. This was the second time I had been in the city, but it was practically all new to me, because my first visit had been a rapid journey with my parents, when I was about eight, to see Pedro, who was just beginning his course in architecture at the time.

A walk through Madrid with Santiago Escrivá

Santiago made no difficulties whatever, and we went out straight away. Among other places, he took me to see the part of the university campus which had been a battle-scene only about a month before. There were zones which could already be visited, because army experts had combed through them and removed the mines and other explosive devices. I was thrilled to be able to get right into the trenches and shelters of the soldiers on the opposing sides, sometimes incredibly close to each other, and their positions totally entangled. When night began to fall he took me to Toledo Street where my aunt and uncle lived. I never forgot this kindness on Santiago's part.

More than fifty years later, in 1991 or 1992, I don't remember exactly when, they told me that Santiago had been taken into Pamplona University Hospital. The last time I had seen him had been in 1955, in Salto di Fondi, a farming estate halfway between Rome and Naples,[7] where I stayed with him and his sister Carmen for long stretches. Half a century had gone by since our first meeting and thirty-five years since our last, and I felt a great need to thank him for very many things, but perhaps especially for taking me round Madrid immediately

---

[7] Salto di Fondi was originally a vast estate belonging to the Marquis of Bisletti. In about 1952 Blessed Josemaría realised the need to provide the many students at the Roman College of the Holy Cross (an international centre of studies of the Work, where over a hundred members from several different countries were already living, most of us quite young) with a place where we could continue studying during the summer months while at the same time "re-oxygenating", as the Father put it; and also a place to hold retreats, courses and other activities. At about the same time he heard that the marquis wished to sell this estate and move to another in Kenya. After long negotiations undertaken by Don Alvaro del Portillo, a cooperative was set up consisting of lots of small-holders, most of them being the actual people who farmed the land. A management committee was set up, and through this roundabout method, a trust was constituted as one of the small-holders, which offered Opus Dei the use of a small part of the estate, including the old house where the marquis's family had lived, for educational purposes. The problem was that there was no money to adapt the house to accommodate the women of Opus Dei in separate and independent quarters so that they could look after the catering and domestic work. The whole process looked like it was going to be a lengthy one. The Father asked Carmen and Santiago to move there for a time in order to set up this activity. Once again, Blessed Josemaría's sister and brother acceded heroically to his request: Santiago Escrivá temporarily left his lawyer's practice in Madrid and Carmen left her home to make a big, ill-proportioned and poorly-furnished house fit for a large number of people to live in. During the academic year 1954-55, while I was doing my doctoral thesis in Theology, I and Don Ramón Bosch, who was doing one in Canon Law, took it in turns a week at a time to go and celebrate Mass and administer the sacraments for the people of the Work there and a large proportion of the farm-workers from that estate and neighbouring ones. This was the last time I had the chance to stay with Aunt Carmen and Uncle Santiago.

after the Civil War. Santiago was in his hospital room with Yoya, his wife, whom I had not met before. Rather abruptly, after our very warm greetings and introductions, I said to Santiago something like, "By the way, Santiago, I've never yet thanked you for that afternoon in May 1939 when you were kind and patient enough to show me round Madrid."

Santiago did not remember. I started reminding him about it in great detail. Suddenly Yoya began to laugh uproariously, and we asked her why.

"You cannot imagine," she answered, "how funny your conversation sounds. I mean, after more than half a century, this gentleman is determined to thank you" – she turned to her husband – "effusively, for an afternoon when you took him to see Madrid. You don't realise the faces you are each making as he tries to make you remember what happened to you both in a couple of hours more than fifty years ago."

From outside our conversation must have sounded really funny. The fact was that I had often heard Blessed Josemaría quote the saying, "Gratitude is a mark of true nobility", and I had waited for years for a chance to repay Santiago in some way for so many kindnesses, which I had never thanked him for. So we enjoyed ourselves very much. At the end of our conversation I had the satisfied feeling of a mission accomplished.

General impression of the day

This was the course of events on that day early

in May 1939 when I first met Blessed Josemaría. At the time my idea of Opus Dei was still somewhat superficial. But the impression made on me was unforeseeably deep. Those people, each so different from the other, whom I had only just met, had offered me straightforward friendliness as though I had known them all my life. It was something new and unimaginable for me. I began to get a glimpse of what the atmosphere might have been like in the Ferraz Residence which Pedro had moved into at the end of 1935 and which he had so often spoken to me about. Years later, recalling that day and other subsequent episodes, I pondered on how much Blessed Josemaría was helped in carrying out the Work God had entrusted to him by the delicate, effective, and varied contribution offered by his mother, sister, and brother.

Of all that I brought away with me from that visit to the St Elizabeth Foundation, what stood out was the impression made on me by the Father, who far surpassed the idea I had formed of him previously. I could not now put into words what I experienced. Obviously, he offered me unlimited trust and sincere affection, for just two reasons, as far as I could see: first, because he was a priest and had to treat everyone with the same friendliness; secondly, because I was Pedro's brother. In short, it was an unforgettable meeting, which I often remembered with pleasure, and which was to have a decisive influence on the rest of my life.

A couple of days later Pedro and I continued our

journey to Calatayud, so I could use the remaining days of the school year for study, before going on holiday as usual to Torrevieja, where the summer holiday atmosphere was not conducive to study. But my encounter at the St Elizabeth Foundation wrought a deep change in the way I took up my life during the summer months, in the gentle and relatively easy-going atmosphere of Los Hoyos.

Pedro Casciaro, father of José María and Pedro, in 1936 just prior to the start of the Spanish civil war.

Emilia Casciaro, mother of José María and Pedro, in the summer of 1939.

South façade of the manor house on the Casciaro estate called *Los Hoyos* in Torrevieja, south-east Spain. The second balcony on the left is that of the bedroom and study which Pedro and José María used in the early months of the Spanish civil war.

Turrets at *Los Hoyos* where water tanks for the estate were located. The Union Jack flew from here.

Chapter Three

Lights in the post-war months
(May – December 1939)

Calatayud: May – June

It was still the early part of May 1939 when I arrived in Calatayud with Pedro. The National Ministry of Education had decreed that secondary school students who had passed their exams at the end of a full year of study in the Republican zone had to have those subjects re-validated. This affected me: I had completed years three and four in the Albacete Institute. I had not completed the fifth year, since the Republican zone had collapsed into confusion in March as the National troops advanced. Pedro, my mother, and I agreed that I should go with him to Calatayud to study for the convalidating exams, before going to Torrevieja in the summer. And that is what I did. I stayed for a long month and a half in Calatayud, as a boarder at the Marist Brothers' school.

The boarding school was a good experience for me. They were celebrating our Lady's month with great devotion. This celebration was one of the things that was new to me. The painful events of the war, my father's exile, and my recent meeting with Blessed Josemaría all put me in the right frame of mind to benefit from the atmosphere of piety fostered by the Marists. I still treasure the memory of those Rosaries and songs to our Lady in the school chapel. I went to some of third- and fourth-year classes at the Calatayud Institute of Secondary Education, where Pedro was teaching mathematics, combining this job with his military duties at the Eastern Provinces Army GHQ. The Principal of the school directed my revision for the convalidating exams I had to take, sometimes giving me private tutorials. He was very kind to me.

When I got a day off school, if Pedro was not taken up with his military duties, I used to go out with him and Pedro de Ybarra[1] to stroll around, have lunch, and talk. Between them, the two Pedros were in sole charge of the Cipher Office,[2] which belonged to the Second Division[3] of the Eastern Provinces Army GHQ: "the Cipher gentlemen", as General Orgaz used to call them with obvious respect; he was the army chief and held them in great esteem for the competence with which they did their work, and their personal qualities.

It must have been at the beginning of June when

---

[1] Pedro de Ybarra was born in Bilbao in 1913. He was Count of Guell and Marquis of MacMahon. When Opus Dei began activities in Bilbao, Pedro de Ybarra helped generously, with the invaluable cooperation of his mother, Carolina ("Carito") MacMahon, Marchioness of MacMahon, who later joined the Work. Pedro did not belong to Opus Dei; he was a loyal friend and cooperator. He died in 1993.

[2] The Cipher Office was the translation bureau for coded orders from the military commanders.

[3] The Second Division was the Military Intelligence Service of the General Staff.

the GHQ was moved to Valencia, and with it both Pedros, so that I was left on my own. But it was for a very short time; at the end of June school broke up for the holidays and I left Calatayud.

Torrevieja again

I then went to Torrevieja for the summer, as was our family custom and because my mother was there. On the way there I stopped for a day or two in Valencia. It was an interesting break: I met Ricardo Fernandez Vallespín,[4] a lieutenant in the Engineers and not yet demobilised, and Amadeo de Fuenmayor.[5] I also spent time with Pedro de Ybarra and, of course, with my brother. We went to Mass in a church I don't remember and had breakfast in a café in what was then called the Plaza de España. I stayed

---

[4] Ricardo Fernandez Vallespín was one of the first members of the Work, which he joined in 1933. He was born in 1910. He took his Architecture degree in Madrid before the Civil War and was apparently younger than anyone in his own year and even in the year below. Blessed Josemaría made him director of the residence at 50 Ferraz Street. He worked as an architect for many years, with his own studio. He was ordained to the priesthood in 1949 and sent by the Founder of Opus Dei to Argentina in 1950, being one of the people who began the apostolate of the Work in that country. From 1962 onwards he exercised his ministry in Madrid. He died in 1988 after a long illness.

[5] Amadeo de Fuenmayor Champín was born in 1915. He was one of the first people to join the Work in Valencia after the war. A renowned practitioner of civil law, he was appointed Professor of Civil Law at the University of Santiago de Compostela in 1943. He had his own legal practice and is a member of the Royal Academy of Juridical and Moral Sciences. He was ordained a priest in 1949 and became an expert in canon law too; he has been dean of the Faculty of Canon Law at the University of Navarre. He is an Honorary Prelate of the Pope. After living for some years in Rome he has now returned to Pamplona.

the night in the boarding house where my brother was living. It was another unforgettable day in the company of "Pedro's friends", as my mother soon began to call them, whom I found it so easy to get on with because they radiated friendliness and peace. I resumed my journey in the dilapidated buses which had survived the war, changing at Alicante, and got to Los Hoyos, where the whole Casciaro clan was waiting for me.

Life there was in a way a repeat of the summer holidays before the war, but with notable and rather painful absences. In the first place, my father was in exile in Oran, and we were only just beginning to receive regular letters from him. His news was good, given his situation. That summer a French couple, Mr and Mrs Martin, both professors at the Lycée (he was Professor of Geography and History, like my father, and she was Professor of Latin), generously offered hospitality to Don Pedro in their own house and treated him as befitted a fellow-professor. There were other absences from Los Hoyos among the older generation; several cousins were not coming for different reasons. My former little gang was considerably diminished.

Pedro was not coming either, as he had in former years, to spend the holidays there and take part in his usual water-sports. He only made two flying visits for specific purposes. I often used to remember the war months and how well-organised my elder brother had been, and I tried to imitate him.

Greater devotion at Los Hoyos

However, there was an exciting difference: my grandfather Julio, who for many years had been cool and critical towards religion, was changing rapidly and radically. The events of the war and its consequences, including the loss of a good part of his property, the exile of his two remaining sons (my father and my uncle Julio, whom the uprising caught in Cartagena where he was the Popular Front Mayor), and the imprisonment awaiting trial of his son-in-law Anastasio, whom he was deeply fond of, were circumstances God made use of – in my mother's and my own opinion – to bring him back to Himself. After many years he had gone to confession to the archpriest Don Benito, the old parish priest at Torrevieja, who, astounded, had ministered to him with great wisdom. My grandfather donated the church vestments from the shrine at Los Hoyos to the parish church, which was then in the process of being rebuilt.

My grandfather used to come to Mass with my mother and myself every day. He was not backward in talking about his conversion. Among other devotions, he liked to say the Rosary with my mother, and hold conversations with her about spiritual matters, discussing the works of St Augustine and St Teresa of Avila, their favourite authors at that time. Aunt Carolina, the oldest of my father's generation, often joined us, and my cousin Adelita sometimes came too. The other people on my father's side of the family had also experienced a return to religion in varying degrees.

In his book *Dream and your dreams will fall short* (pp. 183-4), my brother tells how, when they got to Lourdes after their journey over the Pyrenees, before beginning the Mass of thanksgiving, which Pedro was serving, Blessed Josemaría turned to him and said, "I suppose you will be offering up this Mass for the conversion of your father and for our Lord to grant him many years of life as a Christian." We did not yet know the fruit of Blessed Escrivá's concern for my father's spiritual health, but "God, who never lets himself be outdone in generosity,"[6] had already started on "one of his specialities":[7] not just my father, but my grandfather too, had begun to be converted.

I remember that during this period, talking about the troubles of the war and the good changes, genuine conversions to God on the part of some people at Los Hoyos, my mother said to me one day, "Your brother has brought light to this family." In the few brief meetings we had with Pedro that summer, we learnt little by little about the part Blessed Josemaría's prayer and mortification had played in those conversions in the Casciaro family. As time went by and different things happened I discovered progressively more about Blessed Josemaría Escrivá's big-heartedness. At the same time God gave me great faith in him and granted me other graces, which

---

[6] A phrase I often heard from Blessed Josemaría.
[7] Another phrase I sometimes heard Blessed Josemaría employ.

started to prepare my soul to respond to the divine call to Opus Dei. The reader will forgive these personal notes, which I have often reflected on since then and which, as I write them down, lead me once again to the memory of and the deepest gratitude to God and Blessed Josemaría. Even at that time we could see God's loving hand in the midst of the sufferings brought about by the Civil War and its effects. Later on, when I often heard the Founder of Opus Dei saying that "God writes straight with crooked lines", I would remember the happenings of the war and the changes for the better in people.

Well-planned summer holidays

At Los Hoyos, then, I found the atmosphere very different from what it had been in previous years. That summer Pedro's lightning journeys from Valencia or Madrid enabled him to discuss the whole situation in depth with my mother, my grandfather, and with me as well. He lent me a book which did me a lot of good and influenced my subsequent decision: *Don Bosco and his times*, by Hugo Wast. In those circumstances it was not difficult for me to organise things so as not to waste time as I had before. When we came home from Mass in the hospital chapel – the rebuilding of the parish church and "The Shrine", which had been burnt down in 1936, had not yet been completed – I spent a certain amount of time studying the subjects for my convalidation exams and then went swimming or canoeing with some of my cousins.

The beaches at Torrevieja had a well-behaved, family atmosphere. Today's tourist explosion had not yet taken place. The town council had set up a patrol: a couple of the town guards strolled peaceably along the beaches and rocks safeguarding "good behaviour". We used to call them "Morality". When word went round, "Morality's coming!" everyone would check their beachwear to ensure it was legal and decent, and avoid being fined – it was a token fine, and I do not remember anyone actually being given one.

In the afternoon we would all sit chatting for a little while over the lunch-table in the shade of the east-facing side of the house, where there was a cool breeze from the sea at that time of day. Then I went back to my school-books and spiritual books. There was still time to get on Pedro's old bicycle, then one of my favourite sports, or to do the odd errand driving a cart that belonged to my grandfather, pulled by a spirited but well-trained pony. My meetings in Madrid, Calatayud, and Valencia, and my stay in the Marist school, had given me an idea of piety and the beginnings of an ordered lifestyle. My mother helped me discreetly, without overwhelming me, as she had agreed with Pedro. She made things easier for me and encouraged me to keep up my practices of Christian piety, and my studying. She also gave me sound advice regarding my contacts with girls.

Throughout the summer of 1939 in Torrevieja my desire to get closer to God was growing greater. It was like a small flame which acquired substance in the course of those months. It took no definite shape; just the idea that God was calling me for himself. As the weeks went by it also became progressively clearer to me that what God was asking of me involved a complete giving of myself to him exclusively. Without many more details, I began to comprehend that this kind of divine call brought with it, in the elementary language which I used with myself, the fact of not getting married. And as a result, I had to start by keeping my relations with girls on the sober side. In the first place, by giving up going to the popular evening dances on the Marine Parade, which in those days had a good tone and whole families used to go to them; but they began to seem inappropriate for me. In the second place, it didn't make sense for me to have a steady girlfriend, although there were two girls whom I liked a lot. This sort of attitude required an effort, but it was very clear in my mind and I began to move slowly in that direction. I did not speak of it to anyone, however, apart from one or two conversations with my mother.

I think the reason for my rather elementary level of approach was that my religious upbringing had been quite scanty: except for the month and a half at Calatayud, I had never been to a school run by religious, only to lay schools. My first primary school in Albacete was a private school belonging to a good family man, Don Macedonio Jiménez Maestre, a devout Catholic. For my First Communion I only had a fortnight's preparation at this school, rapidly learning the elementary catechism in a class taken by lay teachers. Incidentally, some prominent right-wingers stupidly poured scorn on my father's decision to celebrate my First Communion. One of them published an article in one of the local dailies under the heading "Laicism, but not in my family", which wounded my parents deeply, and myself as well. My brother was partly saved in those days of bitterness because he had moved to Madrid shortly before to start studying for the School of Architecture entrance examination. After that I went to what was called a Preparatory School, adjoining the Institute of Secondary Education, for the year leading up to the entrance examination for the institute. So that almost all I knew of religion and the practice of Christian piety up till that point was what I had been taught by my mother and later by my brother. Nor did I have a fixed priest for confession; still less did I have a spiritual director. In a sense this role had been fulfilled lately by my mother and my brother.

My father had never raised any difficulties about religious teaching in the heart of his family. He had in fact helped it, by never undermining my mother's authority, but by actually supporting her in this respect. During the Civil War my father even consented without hesitation to having the Blessed Sacrament kept in his house. Don Joaquín Sánchez told my mother that the church authorities in Albacete considered that our house was the safest place for the Blessed Sacrament to be kept, because my father's political situation offered the greatest protection. My mother spoke to my father, and for nearly two years the Blessed Sacrament was reserved in a little cupboard in a sitting-room which was kept locked for the whole period (the cupboard, a very elegant rococo one, is now in a sitting-room at 14 Diego de León Street, in Madrid). They granted my mother permission to take Communion herself every day if she wished to, and so she did. Don Joaquín would come periodically to bring new consecrated hosts. From time to time he came to take Communion to other people.

Jenner Residence opens

Towards the end of July I made a brief journey to Madrid, on my mother's instructions, to ask Pedro's advice on several points. There the first steps were being taken to set up the residence for university students at 6 Jenner Street. I met Francisco Botella, wearing a pale yellow striped shirt, and with a hammer in his hand. I had heard a lot about him as Pedro's inseparable companion in his architecture and mathematics courses, and as one of the residents at Ferraz in the year 1935-36, but I had never met him. We were both very happy to meet. I stayed with my Uncle Mariano and Aunt Juana, as I had at the beginning of May.

My next stay in Madrid, around the middle of August, was a little longer. I spent the night in Jenner. I had asked to be woken up in time to go to Mass in the residence, but no one woke me. By the time I was dressed they were already coming out of the Oratory. As I was explaining that I did not know my way around the neighbourhood, someone told me not to worry, because Alvaro del Portillo was just about to arrive and I could easily go to Mass with him. And so it turned out. In came an Engineering Lieutenant, a strong-looking man with a frank smile, and we went to the church of San Fermín de los Navarros, a Franciscan church which was close by. We went back to Jenner for breakfast. This was another great meeting for me: Alvaro treated me with tremendous affection.[8]

That visit was also quite a short one, to sort out some family matters with Pedro and come to a final

---

[8] It seems almost superfluous for me to include a biographical note here on Bishop Alvaro del Portillo y Diez de Sollano, since he is so well known. He was born in Madrid on 11 March 1914. He obtained three doctorates: in Civil Engineering, Humanities, and Canon Law. He joined the Work in July 1935. From 1939 onwards he was an absolutely faithful collaborator with Blessed Josemaría, being, in Don Alvaro's own phrase, "like his shadow", and remained at his side until Blessed Josemaría went to heaven in 1975. He was ordained to the priesthood in 1944. In 1946 he went to live in Rome, as did the Founder of the Work. He was Consultor to several Congregations of the Roman Curia and took an active part in the work of the Second Vatican Council. On 15 September 1975 he was elected as the Father's first successor. In 1982 Pope John Paul II established the Work as a Personal Prelature, appointing Alvaro del Portillo Prelate of Opus Dei, and on 6 January 1991 the Holy Father consecrated him bishop. Monsignor del Portillo's pastoral government was characterised above all by his fidelity to the message and spirit of Blessed Josemaría. He spread the apostolate of the Work to many new countries. During his governance, on 17 May 1992, Pope John Paul II beatified the Founder of the Work, Monsignor Josemaría Escrivá. He died suddenly on 23 March 1994. On that same day the Holy Father came to pray before his body, which now rests in the crypt of the prelatic church of Opus Dei.

decision about whether to sit for the extra examinations to convalidate the two years' schooling I had done during the war at the Abacete Institute, and the special exam for the year which had been broken off half-way through when the war ended. On journeys of this kind I began to get to know "Pedro's friends", as Doña Emilia called them. I liked the atmosphere in Jenner more and more.

Shortly after this I went to Albacete. The final exams for the first two years went very well. But people were generally very pessimistic about the year which had been left unfinished. The teachers themselves advised us not to take the exam, because it would be almost impossible for us to pass. I telephoned Pedro for advice, and he told me I should definitely take it. I obeyed. The failure rate was indeed extremely high. I was one of only two who passed in every subject. So I regained my proper place in the educational system, instead of having the fifth year hanging over me for an indefinite period as I would have had if I had not taken the exam. Once again I experienced for myself the benefits of following my brother's judgement.

Studying in Barcelona

Because of my father's exile in Oran, obtaining a good education for me was not going to be a straightforward matter. My paternal grandparents (my maternal grandparents had died many years before) lost a lot of their property and businesses in the reverses of the Civil War. In addition, three of their married children had been left in very precarious situations, as I mentioned earlier. My grandparents had to help their grandchildren in all three families, and had to do it fairly. This meant that they could offer to put me up, feed me, and supply me with a modest amount of money, but it would not have been right for them to pay for me to live on my own in another town where there was an Institute of Secondary Education. I would have to study in Torrevieja and take my exams as an independent candidate at Albacete, or else at Orihuela or Alicante. After various family negotiations, we decided the best thing to do would be to accept a generous offer from Diego Ramírez, my mother's only surviving brother, and move to his house in Barcelona. So I did the whole of my sixth year of secondary school in Barcelona, in 1939-40.

Uncle Diego, a devout Catholic and a good journalist, editor of *El Correo Catalan* ("The Catalan Post") and president of the Barcelona Press Association, held me in such affection that he later suggested that I should go to university in Barcelona, living in his house and at his expense. But in practice, it would have been virtual adoption. This was perhaps because my uncle was the only man in his house, having four daughters, all younger than me, and had by now given up hope of having a son; he may have found in me something that he needed psychologically. We certainly had plenty of tastes in common:

we both liked international politics and history, drama, literature, bull-fighting, and everything to do with the sea, because we had both grown up in Torrevieja; and perhaps more than anything else, we loved football. His wife, my Aunt Pilar, was also very fond of me. So that we all got on very well together. But Uncle Diego had a somewhat demanding personality. For this reason my mother and Pedro were very doubtful about his offer to let me stay in his house till I had finished my university studies. The decision did not need to be made immediately. The matter could wait until the beginning of summer 1940.

Decisive encounter with Opus Dei

The summer of 1939 had been an intense one and had brought me into frequent contact with the professional and apostolic activity of some of the faithful of Opus Dei. The small, uncertain flame of dedication to God began to be more clearly defined. What I had seen in the Founder of the Work and in those other men sank in more and more deeply. The virtues I saw in them were an external sign of their internal dispositions of generosity in responding to God's grace. So much seemed obvious to me. In them I thought I could see the characteristics of the response to God that I felt inside myself. And in this way the idea was born that the Work was the path God was calling me to.

A very good understanding existed between my mother and my brother on how to further my education on the human and professional level, and my life of piety. The last meetings between them had given Pedro the chance to explain some aspects of Opus Dei to her. Seeing her oldest son's good example in practice, her liking for the Father and the Work increased progressively, and she told me I should take my brother as my model, with which I entirely agreed. I also received sound help from Uncle Diego, who was a Christian of profound piety and apostolic zeal (as well as the jobs I have mentioned, he had been elected president of the men's branch of Catholic Action in Barcelona). And above all, my meeting with the Founder of the Work in May had made a deep and lasting impression on me.

In the course of the past years Pedro had offered up a great deal of prayer and mortification for me, and generously devoted both human and supernatural care to me. It is not unreasonable to suppose that God our Lord had heard him and prepared my soul gradually with his grace. With great difficulty, in the middle of the changing circumstances of the war and its aftermath, I had moved from a state of being distant from religion to a life more in accordance with what Christian existence should be: practices of piety, spiritual reading and orderly study. The Father too, as a priest, had cared for my brother's family and prayed a lot for my father and me, as he had already told me when I met him in the Royal Foundation of St Elizabeth at the beginning of May 1939. Finally, I think that God also makes use of such serious events as a war

Emilia, with her sons José María (left) and Pedro, in Barcelona (April 1940)

Torrevieja, July 1942: José María Casciaro.

Jenner Residence, in Madrid, occupied part of the first floor and all of the third. This photograph was taken relatively recently.

Madrid, August 1947: Pedro Casciaro, with his son José María, Emilia and Agustín Tomas Moreno (right). It was Agustín who had persisted in trying to introduce José María's older bother, Pedro, to Blessed Josemaría Escrivá.

to make people face up to the mysteries of life and death more deeply and, as in my own case, to enable them to mature more quickly than in peacetime.

Conversation with Pedro at Torrevieja

Things were at this stage when I went back to Torrevieja for the Christmas holidays of 1939-40. Pedro only came for a day or two, just enough to explain the Work to me in all its inmost reality. He lent me a copy of *The Way*, which had been published in Valencia three months before, in September. We spoke at great length and went over my practices of piety and my plan of study. We agreed that I was to think over all the things we had talked about. When I returned to Barcelona, one or other of his friends would get in touch with me so that I could tell him what I had decided; there was no need to hurry things. Pedro did not want to take a hand in my decision, because he was my elder brother, and he wanted me to be able to act with the utmost freedom and with suitable time for thinking things through, without haste.

That long conversation with Pedro made me think a lot. In a way he was giving me a double key: on one hand he was offering the basic reason for the behaviour I had admired in him from the beginnings of the Civil War. On the other hand he was giving me guidance about the impulses I had been feeling in my soul for the past six months.

The divine call is hard to analyse. I have the

vivid memory that an interior force was impelling me, gently but clearly, to give myself to God in Opus Dei, of which I had now acquired a fairly thorough knowledge both in theory and in practice through Pedro's explanations. The key to it, undoubtedly, was the commitment to seek genuine Christian sanctification through study as responsible work, done in God's presence. The foundation of the whole of the Christian life was the sense of knowing that I was a son of God, with a mission of service towards others; and the whole thing was to be seen in the setting of the ordinary circumstances of Christian existence, which develops in the middle of the world.

Perhaps the keenest question I faced was that of apostolic celibacy, though I did not use such a technical name for it at that time. I had thought about this before, but now the question was close at hand: no longer an ideal on a far horizon, but a reality plainly to be seen. And the facility with which the heart of a sixteen-year-old inclines towards one or two of the most attractive girls he meets is well known. God's grace made me see, quite clearly, that my path was to choose him, in a divine adventure, over and above any created being. I saw it as an adventure, but at the same time I felt a serene certainty, an inner confidence that can only come from God himself, who gives the call. I think I did not find it very difficult to get used to the idea of total self-giving and decide on it freely, without any kind of trauma, though I was conscious that that decision implied something very serious. And every time I thought over my choice – to say yes to God's call – I felt a little afraid but very happy inside.

Pedro went straight back to Madrid. I stayed at Torrevieja for Christmas, thinking over all the things we had talked about. I meditated on the points of *The Way* in the tranquil holiday atmosphere. I thought I could take the decisive step soon, when I got back to Barcelona. Before I left Torrevieja I made up my mind seriously to lead a Christian life fully consistent with the demands God was making of me, which I could see more and more clearly. Perhaps because of my youthful impatience, I did not reckon with the fact that the people in Opus Dei would make me wait for several months to consider my attitude.

Chapter Four

Time to decide
(January – July 1940)

Return to Barcelona

From my point of view, the prospects for my joining the Work looked perfectly straightforward, but I had to wait. I had seen that Pedro was not in any hurry; rather the opposite. When the Christmas holidays were over I went back to Barcelona. Probably at the end of January or in February 1940 Amadeo de Fuenmayor arrived and looked me up, but found me in bed with a temperature, caused by a liver infection. My mother had come to Barcelona a few days before to look after me. The three of us were there in my room. Doña Emilia obviously had no idea that Amadeo and I could have any particular matter to discuss. She did not leave us alone for even a minute, because she was delighted by Amadeo's conversation. At one point she offered to get us some tea, and he accepted gratefully, mentioning that he was actually quite hungry after his journey, perhaps in the hope that in the meanwhile we might be able to talk. But she was so quick that in the twinkling of an eye she was back in with the tea, when we had hardly started talking. So in the end his time ran out before we had had the chance to finish our conversation. He left without my having explained to him my decision about the Work. Amadeo had not shown any signs of haste either. When we said goodbye, perhaps noting some evidence of impatience on my part, he said that there would be other opportunities to talk the matter over.

Alvaro del Portillo and my mother

It must have been more or less a month later that Alvaro del Portillo arrived. He waited in Uncle Diego's house, talking with my mother, and both tried to contact me. I was in class at the time and they did not manage to get hold of me. When I came home for lunch I found my mother looking very moved. She could not summarise for me the gist of her long conversation with Alvaro, whom she had not met before. I never learnt what Alvaro had told her, but my mother ended up by saying to me, almost in these exact words, "I don't know what it is about your brother's friends, but I would like you to be like them." Naturally, I did know what it was. Anyway, with the sixth sense that mothers have about what is good for their children, Doña Emilia clearly perceived how very sensitively and supernaturally Pedro's friends spoke and acted.

Alvaro's journey was a rapid one, and I was not able to see him. I had missed another chance of telling someone about my decision. So I just had to be patient. Perhaps, in God's providence, it was better if my decision had time to mature because of those unexpected difficulties, which seemed to me to be merely holding things up.

Pedro in Barcelona again

Pedro came in April. He stayed for several days, because he had a very important matter to deal with: after many difficulties he had managed to get a visa from the French Embassy in Madrid for my mother to go to Oran. For months my father had been saying in his letters that he was unwell, and we could tell that he was sad. My mother decided that her mission at that time was to go and join him in exile. He needed her more than her children did, since our prospects, thank God, looked very promising. Pedro and I supported her in her decision. My mother's journey was a somewhat heroic one, from Barcelona to Madrid, from there to (what was at that time) the Spanish Protectorate of Morocco, and then, in a series of buses, on to Oran, often with Moroccan or Algerian men for her only travelling companions. During these last stages of the journey she was really frightened. When my father saw her arrive he was so overjoyed he could scarcely believe it was true.

But let us return to Barcelona. On several days Pedro and I talked in depth and at great length. Although as far as I was concerned everything was absolutely clear, Pedro told me that the Father had reminded him that, as we were brothers and he was quite a bit older than me – those eight and a half years, naturally, were still between us – they were not going to treat my reply as final, because they wanted to be sure that it was an absolutely free decision. To me this looked like yet another delay. It was not really like that. For one thing, I was still a few months short of my seventeenth birthday. For another, the people in Opus Dei wanted to be certain of the firmness and constancy of my decision, as with everyone else. So there was no hurry. The only person in a hurry was myself. As will shortly be seen, the way things turned out was much better.

Pedro introduced me to Rafael Termes,[1] who was twenty-two and almost at the end of his degree in Industrial Engineering, and who had been in the Work for only a few weeks. He was a friendly and intelligent person whom I found it easy to talk to sincerely about everything I was feeling. We agreed to meet frequently. And so we did. Rafael, despite having been in the Work for such a short time, was fully able to explain to me some points concerning the spirit of Opus Dei, zeal for holiness and apostolate, and so on. I found our conversations extremely useful and encouraging.

The Father was expected in Barcelona shortly. When he came I would have the chance to speak to

---

[1] Rafael Termes Carrero, as is well known, is brilliant in his profession. He went into business management, economics, and banking. He became president of AEB (*Asociación Española de Banca*, the Spanish Banking Association) and until his recent retirement fulfilled this role to everyone's satisfaction.

the Founder of Opus Dei directly and, if I wanted, explain my dispositions to him with regard to my decision. Meanwhile, I had to keep on waiting.

I ask the Father to admit me into the Work

On 12 May, while I was having lunch at Uncle Diego Ramírez's house, Rafael telephoned to say that the Father was in Barcelona and I could see him at the Urbis Hotel in Gracia Walk. The wave of emotion that swept over me may easily be imagined. I finished my lunch hastily and said good-bye to the family. It was a Sunday. That was the day when I usually went to watch a football match with Uncle Diego; we used to walk from Urquinaona Square, where we lived on the corner of Layetana Way, to the Las Corts or Sarria football ground, depending on which of Barcelona's two football teams was playing. We paid close attention to the development of the game; we would walk back home (this walk was our main opportunity for exercise in the week), talking over and analysing the match. When we got home my uncle would dictate the account to Aunt Pilar, and after dinner we took it round to the offices of "The Monday Chronicle" (*La Hoja Oficial del Lunes*) for publication. That particular day, my uncle was getting over influenza and could not go to the match. Taking it for granted that I would go, he warned me as I went out, "Pay attention and take good note of it all, because when you get back we will have to write up the report for the press."

I did not think it was the right moment to object, and without thinking too much about it I rushed out to the Urbis Hotel; I would see about solving the problem of the match report later.

Blessed Josemaría received me straight away. As at our first meeting – it was a year since that day in May 1939 – he treated me with great warmth. He asked me some questions to see whether I had thoroughly understood what the calling to the Work means. My answers seemed to satisfy him. Then he asked me, very seriously, "Has your brother Pedro put pressure on you?"

He asked me the same question in different ways twice more. I remember getting quite anxious, because it almost began to seem as if he was not going to take account of my request, which I had held inside myself for nearly five months now. I no longer remember the way I explained myself, but what I said must have made enough sense for Blessed Josemaría to be sure that my decision was completely free and well thought over, because he said finally, "Consider yourself in the Work. Go and have a talk with Alvaro now, and he will explain a few things to you."

My joy, and relief even, can easily be imagined: at last my long-standing desire was fulfilled, my long-cherished dream was a reality. All this was something tremendous for me. Perhaps I do not need to clarify that asking to be admitted to the Work is not the same thing as belonging to Opus Dei juridically. At least a year and a half must go by to become a member, in law. But the Work offers everyone appropriate means for their ascetical and human formation and their training in religious doctrine, just as it does to those who are, legally speaking, members of Opus Dei; and it shows the same care and attention to everyone. Because of this, from the first moment we feel that we are in the Work, with the full trust of children with their own family, living in a spirit of filiation towards the Father and fraternity towards the other faithful of Opus Dei.

Later, when I recalled that meeting with the Founder of the Work, I understood the exquisite care Blessed Josemaría took of people's freedom in giving themselves to God, so that this self-giving was made sincerely and for supernatural reasons alone. When I heard him say, on various occasions, that in Opus Dei we have a narrow door by which to get in and a wide one for leaving, I always remembered that episode on 12 May 1940, which confirmed the profound truth of this statement.

I went off and had a good long talk with Alvaro. He explained more to me about aspects of life in the Work. He revised my programme of practices of piety, starting from what I was already doing habitually. He specified the time I should spend in mental prayer and gave me some advice on how to do it. He gave me words of encouragement and, finally, advised me to talk to Rafael Termes regularly, so that he could guide me in whatever things I needed help with on this new stage I was undertaking.

José Luis Múzquiz,[2] a civil engineer, and Juan Jiménez Vargas,[3] a doctor, had also come with the Father. I had not met them before, and they seemed a lot older than me, both being twenty-eight. I had a

---

[2] José Luis Múzquiz de Miguel, who had been a civil engineer since before the Spanish Civil War, later obtained a doctorate in humanities. He was one of the first people to join the Work when the war ended. He was ordained a priest in 1944, together with Alvaro del Portillo and José María Hernández de Garnica. He soon turned out to be one of the Father's greatest helpers and was entrusted by him with some very responsible apostolic tasks, including being Counsellor for the region of Spain. Later, in 1949, he became the first Counsellor for the United States. He died there in 1983 with a reputation for holiness. I remember him as a tireless worker, completely dedicated to God and sacrificing himself entirely for his brothers.

[3] Juan Jiménez Vargas had been in the Work since January 1933. When the Spanish Civil War broke out he had just got his degree in Medicine and Surgery. He had been an intern in the physiology department run by Dr. Negrín, who was President of the Council of Ministers of the Republic during the conflict. Juan Jiménez, after crossing over to the Nationalist zone, was an army doctor at the battle-front. He obtained the chair of Physiology at the University of Barcelona in 1942. A well-known researcher, he founded the *Spanish Physiological Review*.

He was the first dean of the Faculty of Medicine at the University of Navarre. After prolonged years of illness, borne with heroic humility and a profound understanding and acceptance of suffering and limitation, he died in Pamplona on 29 April 1997, surrounded by very special affection and admiration on the part of his colleagues, friends, and students. Two days later Monsignor Javier Echevarría, the Bishop Prelate of Opus Dei and Chancellor of the University of Navarre, arrived from Rome to preside over the concelebrated Mass offered for the soul of Juan Jiménez. This was celebrated in the university sports stadium, which was filled to capacity (about 4,500 people). For myself, I have to say that I held him in special affection and veneration right from the start because of his human qualities and his loyalty to Blessed Josemaría and the Work, which he maintained in an exemplary way for the almost sixty-five years of his life in Opus Dei. I have no doubt that he was a saint.

chat with José Luis about some of the characteristics and demands of the calling to the Work. I was to have a lot to do with both of them in the years that followed.

Report on a football match

After several hours had gone by at the Urbis Hotel, I suddenly remembered my promise to Uncle Diego about writing up the football match. By that time it was over. I started to feel rather anxious and told Alvaro about it. There were several other students there, including Rafa Escolá[4] and Ramón Guardáns, neither of whom I had met before. Ramón got in touch with a friend of his who was a great football fan. I asked him lots of questions over the telephone about how the match had gone, until I had a fairly complete idea of it. It was getting quite late, and I had to get back to Uncle Diego's house. On the way home I thought over the facts I had been given, and when I got there, without explaining the circumstances, I went through what I thought must have happened on the football field for my uncle, taking care to speak in general terms so that I didn't actually say whether I had seen it or not. Perhaps I should

---

[4] Rafael Escolá was twenty-three at that time. He worked as an industrial engineer in Barcelona and Madrid for several years. He then settled in Bilbao, where he founded and managed a large planning and construction business, which executed major projects in Spain, many of the countries in South America, Pakistan, and others, so that he acquired a tremendous standing on the human and professional level. He died in 1995, surrounded by deep, widespread affection.

explain that Uncle Diego had appointed me unpaid sports correspondent of the *Catalan Post*. That meant that on showing my accreditation I got free entry into the press section of football grounds. In the end we dictated the report to my aunt and then I took it to the newspaper offices. The next day I did not want to see how it looked in print, nor did I bring the subject up. Obviously, I had no wish to go back over the affair. So the days went by until it was all past history. For a time I was afraid that the matter might come up at any moment in conversation, but it seemed as though my uncle did not wish to refer to it either. We never spoke of it again, and I could breathe freely: the mess-up had no repercussions at all.

My brother Pedro

On that 12 May 1940 Pedro, so to speak, handed on the baton to the next runner, meaning myself: he had run an excellent relay race. With the years of prayer and mortification he had offered for me, he had undoubtedly obtained from God the grace of my divine calling: it was the best thing he could possibly do for his brother in this life and for the next. God himself knows how deeply grateful I have always been to Pedro. As I mention the first men I met in my contacts with Opus Dei I have added (and will continue to) a biographical note, so that the reader can have at least a few facts and references. Although to begin with I did not intend to include one about my brother, in the end, now that God our Lord has taken him to heaven, it seems a good idea to do so. A brief biography is included here as a footnote.[5]

The apartment at 62 Balmes Street

After that 12 May, Rafael Termes told me how useful it would be to look for an apartment to be used as the Centre for the apostolic activities which had begun in Barcelona. On a map of the city, he showed me the area where it would be best to have one. We shared this area out between us and began the search. When I came out of classes in the afternoons I would spend one or two hours on this job. Wherever I saw a "To Let" notice, I would go and speak to the porter, who, not necessarily paying me much attention, would give me the information I asked for. After

---

[5] Pedro Casciaro Ramírez was born in Murcia on 16 April 1915. He became a member of Opus Dei on 20 November 1935. He had a doctorate in Mathematics and another in Canon Law. He had already studied the first years of the School of Architecture by 1936. After the Spanish Civil War the Founder of the Work put him in charge of different apostolic activities, like setting up and running the university residences at 16 Samaniego Street in Valencia (1940) and Abando in Bilbao (1944). He was ordained to the priesthood in 1946. In 1948 Blessed Josemaría sent him to visit most of the countries on the American continent, from Canada to Argentina, to make an on-the-spot study of the prospects for Opus Dei to spread there. In January 1949 he went to Mexico to start the apostolic activities there. He stayed in Mexico for about ten years as Counsellor of Opus Dei. Blessed Escrivá then summoned him to Italy, where he stayed for approximately another ten years, first as Procurator of the Work to the Holy See and then as a member of the governing body of Opus Dei in Italy. At the beginning of the 1970s he returned to Mexico, where he continued to exercise his ministry as a priest until his death on 23 March 1995. He was an Honorary Prelate of the Pope.

several such days, I considered that investigations into my area of Barcelona were complete. I gave Rafael a list of the four or five apartments which featured the conditions he had specified. Among these was the one at 62 Balmes Street.[6]

Some days later Rafael told me that we had taken the apartment. It was rented in the name of Alfonso Balcells,[7] the only one of his friends who had already graduated from university, where he had studied medicine. Alfonso was not in the Work but, understanding the situation, willingly allowed his name to be given. We began to use the apartment without a stick of furniture. Rafael soon brought a bed from his parents' house, and one or two other items of furniture as well. I couldn't manage that much. All I brought was a few objects and a map, unframed, about three or four square metres in size, which Uncle Diego had given me. It showed practically the whole of central Europe, and we used to look at it in the hopes that one day, when the Second

---

[6] This apartment in Balmes Street still exists, at the same number, and is still being used for the formative activities of Opus Dei. Therefore it is now the Centre of the Prelature which has been in use the longest. The special affection I feel for that small apartment may easily be understood.

[7] Alfonso Balcells Gorina was born in Barcelona in 1915. For about two years, at the beginning of the 1940's, he endured insults and persecution at the hands of certain religious who thought he was a member of Opus Dei, which they wrongfully accused of being a heretical sect. Alfonso, heroically loyal to his friends in the Work, chose to suffer their slanders in silence. Two years later he asked for admission to Opus Dei. He was Professor of General Pathology at the University of Salamanca, and Rector of the same university from 1960 to 1968. He now lives in Barcelona.

World War was over, some of us would go to those countries to practise our professions and spread the apostolic activities of Opus Dei there. Having nothing else to decorate the house with, we put it up provisionally on the walls of what we planned would be a study-room. The most important contribution to the house was the arrival of two tables and six chairs so that we could work there, and a wooden cross,[8] which Rafael had had made and which was placed in the room which was to be the Oratory. So, little by little, in great poverty as usual, the rooms began to be furnished provisionally.

And the activities started up in the apartment, which we jokingly called *El Palau*, "The Palace". At the beginning of July Adolfo Rodríguez Vidal,[9] a

---

[8] Two points from *The Way* illustrate the symbolism of this cross: "When you see a poor wooden Cross, alone, uncared-for, and of no value... and without its Crucified, don't forget that that Cross is your Cross: the Cross of each day, the hidden Cross, without splendour or consolation..., the Cross which is awaiting the Crucified it lacks: and that Crucified must be you." (*The Way*, 178). "You ask me: why that wooden Cross? – And I copy from a letter: 'As I look up from the microscope, my sight comes to rest on the cross – black and empty. That Cross without its Crucified is a symbol. It has a meaning which others cannot see. And though I am tired out and on the point of abandoning the job, I once again bring my eyes to the lens and continue: for the lonely Cross is calling for a pair of shoulders to bear it.'" (*The Way*, 277). Pope Pius XII later granted indulgences to those who kissed it or said a short prayer before it.

[9] Adolfo Rodríguez Vidal worked as a naval engineer for a time and was ordained a priest of Opus Dei in 1948. He went to Chile, where he was Councillor of Opus Dei for many years and exercised an intensive priestly ministry. He was ordained Bishop of Los Angeles, Chile, in 1988, and retired from active ministry in 1994 because of a grave illness.

twenty-year-old from Tarragona, arrived. He had gone to Madrid at the beginning of the 1939-1940 academic year to study for the entrance examinations to the School of Naval Engineering. There he met Gonzalo Ortiz de Zárate,[10] originally from Alava but now living in Madrid, who was two years younger than him and was doing the same course. They soon became friends. Gonzalo, who had recently joined the Work, took Adolfo to the residence at 6 Jenner Street to attend the means of Christian formation given there. At the end of the year Adolfo asked to be admitted to the Work. His arrival made us deeply happy: at that point in time, having one more person in Barcelona meant a great deal to the few of us who were there.

Quick visit from Chiqui

Before we could move into the "The Palace", José María Hernández de Garnica, whom we called by his family nickname, Chiqui, paid us a short visit in Barcelona. It was around the 27th or 28th of May. I had not met him before. I spent a few hours with him. I went around with him as he dealt with various

---

[10] Gonzalo Ortiz de Zárate, a naval engineer, went to Mexico in 1949, one of the first to spread the Work in that country. He worked as an engineer there for several years. He later took a degree in History and taught the subject in Mexico D.F. Suffering from heart disease, he went to Pamplona in Spain in 1975. After an operation at the University Hospital, he was able to return to normal work and became the director of the University of Navarre Information Service. He died, in a thoroughly exemplary Christian way, in 1989.

small matters, but it was enough to enable me to go deeper into some aspects of the spirit of the Work. Naturally, in those weeks I was watching and learning from the people who had already been in the Work for years.

The Father in Barcelona

Very shortly after Adolfo's arrival Blessed Josemaría came to see us in Barcelona alone. It was a quick visit, from 27 to 29 July. He chose to stay at the apartment in Balmes Street, although it was still very scantily furnished, as I have said. He went to see several people, though I do not know whom. The few of us who were already his sons had the chance to talk to him, all together and each in a more personal conversation as well. During that short visit he spoke to us about a life of prayer and the sanctification of work, apostolic spirit, and the meaning of our divine sonship. We had already read and meditated on *The Way*, but the Father's words made it come alive. They filled us with encouragement, as one may well imagine.

To me, at least, he did not talk about the specific reasons for his journey. Years later I learnt something of what had brought him, but this is not the place to go into it, since I did not actually witness any of it. Those reasons belong to one of the hard times in the history of people's misunderstandings of Opus Dei, which its Founder suffered in indescribable charity, patience, and silence. A further reason, and a very important one, for his journey was to spend time with the new sons of his prayer and mortification. Those hours with the Father were something we treasured deeply. A few university students also came to talk to him. He blessed the Balmes Street apartment, wearing vestments and liturgical objects lent by the superior of the Congregation of St Philip Neri, who had been my confessor for some months before.

Alone with the Father from Barcelona to Madrid

Pedro had told the family that he wanted me to join him in Madrid for a time, since for more than a year we had not had the chance to be together except for a few days, and he could not get to Torrevieja. It seemed a good idea for me to go soon, before I joined in the usual family plan of the long summer holidays at Torrevieja. So I now got ready to make the journey to Madrid, since Blessed Josemaría was going back and I could travel with him.

We had to take the night train, leaving at nine in the evening. I do not remember whether it was an express or the mail train. Rafael, Adolfo, and a few others who were interested in the formative activities of the Work came to see the Father off at the station. It was very hot, since it was the end of July. We got there in plenty of time to catch the train. While we were waiting, we sat at the tables of an open-air cafe and had a drink. As heat has never worried me much, I had a hot chocolate, perhaps with *churros* as well. These refreshments were in fact all the Father had for his evening meal that day. My luggage consisted of two suitcases, a big one full of clothes and a small one of books, which weighed as much as the other. The Father was only carrying a briefcase with what he needed for a short visit. He picked up the suitcase of books before I could prevent him, and we boarded the train. Our tickets were for seats in a compartment which of course, at that time of year, was completely full.

"In Madrid, you are to do whatever you like"

When the train had started I asked him, "Father, what can I do in Madrid now?" His reply was swift: he said immediately, "In Madrid, you are to do whatever you like."

I did not actually understand his answer in its fullness. I did not have any plan but was just looking forward to going back to the Jenner Street residence for a few days to be there, quite simply, with the Father, Pedro, and the other people of the Work. Although I did not understand his reply, it made such an impression on me that I have never forgotten it.

Later on I began to understand those spontaneous words. They showed his respect for everyone's freedom, and especially that of his sons in the Work, and also something really admirable, which is the trust the Father had in us. "I trust the word of a son of mine more than the unanimous testimony of a hundred notaries", I was to hear him say on several occasions. Later, too, I was able to appreciate the theological depths of his attitude: he trusted his sons' truthfulness, our integrity in living our lives in God's sight, and the fact that we were seeking the Good for completely supernatural reasons.

From this perspective, I understood that "whatever you like" does not mean doing whatever one happens to fancy, without more ado; it means taking the initiative to aim at the true Good, to choose what an honest, truthful conscience suggests at each moment, without becoming unduly complicated by rules, but taking care to form that conscience in accordance with the truths of the faith. In short, it means doing what is right, out of a conscious decision to do it, because it is what God wants, not because we are forced to or just because we feel like it.

Blessed Josemaría's love for freedom was something that impressed me right from the start. More so, perhaps, at that time, when it was not a subject that was much talked about. Other values were underlined, such as service and sacrifice for one's country, self-denial in suffering, heroism to the point of risking one's life in defence of high ideals, and so on. But I always heard Blessed Josemaría speak of freedom and responsibility; the Christian freedom that Jesus Christ brought us by his redemption, the freedom of those who are and feel that they are God's children; and respect for other people's freedom, a truly deep dimension of the broad spectrum of freedoms.

During that journey from Barcelona to Madrid, we talked a little more after the train started. Not long afterwards they put out the main lights in the compartment and silence fell, because the passengers seemed to be in a hurry to try and get to sleep. I do not know if they managed to, but I did, sitting happily beside Blessed Josemaría. At about five in the morning I woke up. I said to the Father that I would do the half-hour's mental prayer that the members of the Work usually do first thing in the morning. He assented and told me that he had already done it. From our short conversation I gathered that he had also prayed the Breviary and done several other things besides. I thought, "Then, when did the Father sleep?" Our travelling companions in the compartment looked as if they had slept very badly, sitting in their seats.

When I finished my prayer we spoke for a little, about nothing particular, given the crowded state of the railway carriage. That journey was the only one I made on my own with Blessed Josemaría: I never had another chance like it.

In Madrid

We arrived in Madrid on 30 July 1940, at about half past eleven in the morning. Alvaro and Ricardo Fernández Vallespín, both of whom I already knew, were waiting for the Father at Atocha Station. Ricardo was driving a small car, an old black Lancia that he used for his work as an architect. We went to the Jenner Residence, and the Father celebrated Mass immediately. I served the Mass as best I could, since it was only the second time in my life I had done so. When I was not sure, or did something wrong, he indicated what I should do. He did not refer to my ignorance at all afterwards.

On the other hand, many years later, in Rome, when I had been ordained, I was his server when he was consecrating an altar and I also made several mistakes. This time, when we had finished, he reproved me for not having studied the ceremony properly beforehand. He always insisted that we priests should adhere to the rubrics laid down by Church liturgy with loving care. It is yet another way of showing love for our Lord, and another proof of the professional competence all the faithful of the Work should have in their jobs, which in the case of priests is their priestly ministry in all its aspects.

I was looking forward to those days I was going to spend in Madrid with interest. But I did not suspect at the time that my stay there would actually last for twenty-seven years, until 1967, when I moved to Pamplona, except for a month and a bit in 1945 when I went to help in setting up *Carmen de las Maravillas* (the university students' residence in the popular district of Albaycín in Granada); my military service; four years' study in Rome between 1951 and 1955, to take degrees in Theology and Sacred Scripture; and some other short breaks of no particular significance. Obviously, those twenty-seven years in Madrid, in my youth, which lasted a long time, have left their mark very firmly on my character.

Chapter Five

In the heart of the Work
(Jenner, Summer 1940)

Jenner Residence

The residence for university students at 6 Jenner Street represents, to my mind, an important milestone in the history of Opus Dei, as the Centre where a considerable number of members of the Work lived together for the first time. Perhaps it is useful to note here that members of Opus Dei are not obliged to live under the same roof, in the Centres where its formative work is carried out. In fact, most of them live with their families or wherever is most suitable for their job. Only a small proportion live in Centres of the Work, either for the sake of their spiritual or theological training, or for specific needs of the apostolate.

Before the Spanish Civil War, in the old Academy-cum-residence at 48-50 Ferraz Street, there were only three members of the Work living there: Ricardo Fernández Vallespín, who was the director, and my brother and Paco Botella, who were residents there. Blessed Josemaría never actually lived in the Ferraz Street residence, though he spent very many hours there. There was no real unit run by women to look after the domestic work: the Father's mother and sister did not undertake this work in Ferraz, and the women of the Work were not in a position to do it at that time either. There was just one lady who cooked the meals and was in general charge of the housework; and she only worked for a few hours every day.

Most of the material care of the house was seen to by the Founder and the three people I have just mentioned, because there was no money to employ any staff. They themselves got the breakfast, made the beds when the other residents were out, did the housework that was still left undone, and so on. The other young members of the Work, like Juan Jiménez Vargas, Alvaro del Portillo and José María Hernández de Garnica, lived with their families and could only lend a hand from time to time, especially on feast-days and in the holidays, when their academic commitments allowed. Finally, there was a boy who looked after the door and telephone for certain hours every day.

People who lived in Jenner

To begin with, I would say there were about fifty of us. In the first place there was the Founder of Opus Dei, his mother Doña Dolores, and his sister and brother, Carmen and Santiago; and Alvaro del Portillo, who is well known and about whom I have supplied a biographical sketch in a previous footnote.

Justo Martí,[1] a lawyer of twenty-eight, was director of the residence at that stage and was popular with the residents because straight after the Civil War he had been mayor of Oliva, his home town in the province of Valencia. Isidoro Zorzano, an industrial engineer who had been one of the Father's fellow-students at secondary school in Logroño, was administrator of the Work and the residence that summer.

Other residents were Ricardo Fernández Vallespín, an architect; Juan Jiménez Vargas, the doctor; and José María González Barredo,[2] who seemed very old to me, being thirty-four and a professor at the Institute. Then there was my brother Pedro; Francisco Botella; Vicente Rodríguez Casado,[3]

---

[1] Justo Martí Gilabert was a resident at 50 Ferraz Street in 1935-36 while he was studying for competitive examinations for one of the branches of the Law degree. Shortly after he had resigned as mayor of Oliva, Blessed Josemaría appointed him director of the residence in Jenner Street. He was ordained a priest in 1946 and was a member of the Regional Commission of Opus Dei in Spain for several years. He died a holy death in 1988, at the end of a life given wholly to his priestly ministry and the apostolic activities of the Work.

[2] José María González Barredo had met Blessed Josemaría in 1929, when he was a chemistry student. In 1931 he was appointed to the chair of Physics and Chemistry in the National Institute of Secondary Education at Linares, Jaén. He joined Opus Dei on 11 February 1933, a few weeks after Juan Jiménez Vargas. In 1942 he became Professor of Chemistry and Physics at the University of Saragossa. In 1946 he went to the United States, where he helped in the beginnings of the apostolate of Opus Dei. He was a lecturer at Harvard University and Columbia University and a researcher for the National Bureau of Standards. After his retirement he returned to Spain and died in 1993 after a long illness.

[3] Vicente Rodríguez Casado was Professor of Modern and Contemporary History at the University of Seville. He joined the Work in April 1936. With his apostolic drive and his open, friendly character

twenty-three, who was later to found the School of Spanish-American Studies in Seville and the Spanish-American University of La Rábida; José Luis Múzquiz, a civil engineer, whom I have referred to in a previous chapter; Rafael Calvo, a twenty-four-year-old from Valencia; Francisco Ponz,[4] who is held in special affection by all those of us who knew him for many years as Vice-Chancellor of the University of Navarre; Juan Antonio Galarraga,[5] a chemistry and pharmacy undergraduate; Jesús Larralde,[6] nineteen, who was to become a leading pharmacist and dean of the faculty at the University of Navarre. And undoubtedly a few more, whom I no longer remember.

Naturally, there were also other residents who did not belong to Opus Dei then, like Emiliano

---

he was the first instrument to spread Opus Dei in Seville and Western Andalucia, where he brought to the Work men like Florentino Pérez Embid. He helped in the development of the University of Piura in Peru. He wrote some outstanding works of historical research and trained many followers in his field. He died in 1990.

[4] Francisco Ponz Piedrafita was born in Huesca in 1919. He was Professor of Animal Physiology at the University of Barcelona and then at the University of Navarre, where he succeeded Don José María Albareda, whose student he had been, as Vice-Chancellor. He is now Professor Emeritus of the University of Navarre.

[5] Juan Antonio Galarraga Ituarte was born in 1920. He went to England in 1946 to do research in biochemistry. He was the first to begin the activities of Opus Dei there. After being ordained to the priesthood in 1953 and exercising his pastoral ministry in the United Kingdom for many years, he returned to Spain in 1972 where he continues the same mission.

[6] Jesús Larralde Berrio was Professor of Pharmacy at the Universities of Santiago de Compostela and Navarre. He was a prolific research worker, with many followers. He is Professor Emeritus at the University of Navarre, the region where he was born.

Amann, an architectural student who later designed Islabe Conference Centre near Bilbao and joined the Work; Angel Galíndez, who was a student in the School of Agricultural Engineering and, years later, president of the Board of the Bank of Vizcaya; Carlos Arencibia, a chemistry student who was such a good footballer that he later played for Bilbao Atletico as centre-forward, though he was not a professional; Rafael Garamendi, who started off studying for the entrance examination to the School of Architecture and then changed over to Law; Alfredo Carrato, later Professor of Medicine; and some others whose names escape me after half a century; I apologise to them and to my readers.

Three domestic employees, or perhaps more, helped Doña Dolores and Carmen with the cooking and housework; I do not know whether they lived in the residence, but I am inclined to think not. I have sometimes stopped to think about the huge amount of work that Grandmother and Aunt Carmen did in Jenner, with so many men to look after and so few people to help them.

Although it was summer, the residence was almost full. This was because when the Civil War ended the universities had been closed for nearly three years. In order to fill the many gaps left by death and exile in either zone the authorities had arranged that from October 1939 to October 1940 there would be a double year of teaching for all those who had missed their classes.

Naturally, the students had to work through the summer just as hard as they had in winter. In addition, many of them had not yet been discharged from the army and had to combine their studying with military duties. The spectacle of all those university students studying so intensely in the middle of the summer struck me as surprising and even rather funny, since it did not affect me directly. Sometimes I felt sorry for them. One or other of them would say at breakfast that he had sat up all night reading the textbook of the subject for his next examination. They did not need to prove it: the dark circles round their eyes amply confirmed these claims.

People who lived with their families

Finally, there were other people who had asked for admission into the Work after the Civil War and were living at home with their parents. These included Fernando Valenciano,[7] who would become a civil engineer; Salvador Canals,[8] who was to become an Auditor of the Sacred Roman Rota; Gonzalo Ortiz

---

[7] Fernando Valenciano Polack was born in 1922. He was the first person to join Opus Dei in Madrid after the Civil War. After working as an engineer for many years in Spain, he moved to Rome, where he worked closely with Blessed Josemaría in the governance of the Work. He was ordained a priest at the age of seventy and continues to exercise his priestly ministry in the Eternal City.

[8] Salvador Canals Navarrete was born in 1920. He was a lawyer. He went to Rome in 1942. There he obtained a doctorate *"In Utroque Iure"* – in Civil Law and Canon Law – at the Lateran University. He was ordained a priest 1948 and stayed in Rome, where he died in 1975 with a reputation for holiness.

de Zárate, a future naval engineer; José Antonio Sabater, who was a teacher in secondary education for many years;[9] and Alvaro del Amo,[10] who would become an excellent biologist.

All of these people were about the same age, around twenty. Alberto Ullastres[11] had joined the Work in the same period as them, but was five or six years older, and at that stage the difference is a big one.

Someone else who was not living in the Jenner Street residence that summer was José María Hernández de Garnica, who had recently had an operation for the removal of a kidney, damaged in an accident and by his adventures during the Civil War, when he had endured imprisonment and harsh conditions. He was now recovering from the operation, and the Father had suggested that for a time he should stay in his family's house, since Jenner did not offer suitable conditions for his convalescence.

---

[9] José Antonio Sabater was born in 1921. He is one of the teachers who started Gaztelueta School in Bilbao, the first primary and middle school run by faithful of the Work.

[10] Alvaro del Amo was born in Madrid in 1922. He took a doctorate in Natural Sciences, left Spain to further his studies, and then lived in Portugal from 1948 to 1954, where he was among the first people to spread the apostolate of Opus Dei. He then became a lecturer in Genetics at the University of Navarre. He died in 1985.

[11] Alberto Ullastres was born in 1914. He was Professor of History of Economics at the University of Madrid. He is well known as an economist and for having been Minister of Commerce at the end of the fifties and beginning of the sixties. Later he became Spanish Ambassador to the European Economic Community.

From time to time Don José María Albareda[12] was to be seen in the Jenner Street residence. As first general secretary of the Higher Scientific Research Council for many years, he played an important role in promoting scientific research in Spain after the Civil War. He lived in the researchers' residence, known as the El Pinar Residence, in the area known as Altos de Serrano.

Visitors

There were still further reasons why Jenner was full. On the one hand, those who had asked to join Opus Dei outside Madrid during the year 1939-40 did their best to get to the capital to spend time with Blessed Josemaría and live in the atmosphere of Jenner, even if only for a few days. These short stays helped them enormously to deepen in the divine call that they had received.

On the other hand, in the months of August and September the second and third "study weeks" or

---

[12] José María Albareda Herrera was born in Caspe, Saragossa, in 1902. He studied chemistry at Saragossa and pharmacy at Madrid. He was Professor of Agriculture at the Huesca Institute of Secondary Education and then in the Velazquez and Ramiro de Maeztu Institutes in Madrid. He studied at Bonn, Zurich, and Königsberg, specializing in pedology, or study of soils, a science he introduced into Spain. In 1940 he was Professor of Applied Geology in the Faculty of Pharmacy at the University of Madrid. He joined Opus Dei in 1937. He was rector of the University of Navarre. He was ordained a priest and died of a heart attack in 1966, while preaching. The many scientists who knew him stress his special qualities as a scientist and a man, and his great goodness and humility.

"work weeks" – they went by either name – were organised in Jenner. These were courses of formation consisting of classes on the teaching of the Church, the Liturgy, Christian asceticism and the spirit of Opus Dei, as well as readings of different documents written by Blessed Josemaría from the beginning of the Work, with comments and explanations either by himself or by one of those who had been longest in the Work. Sometimes, at nightfall, we would go from one to another of the places which belonged to the recent history of the Work: the house where the DYA Academy had been, on the corner of Luchana Street and Juan de Austria Street; the former sites of the residences at 50 and 16 Ferraz Street; the café called *El Sotanillo*[13] in Alcalá Street, where Blessed Josemaría had sometimes got together with small groups of young men before he acquired a place of his own for these meetings; and the Royal Foundation of St Elizabeth. The church of Our Lady of the Angels[14] would also be included.

---

[13] *El Sotanillo*, or "The Cellar", was so called because it was half underground, reached by a flight of stairs going down from street level. It was in Alcalá Street near Alcalá Gate. It was a pleasant, welcoming place, if modest, its vaulted ceiling showing the structure of the building. In 1940 and for several years afterwards it was still exactly the same as it had been before the Civil War. One of the oldest waiters even remembered Blessed Josemaría coming there occasionally with young men at the beginning of the 1930's.

[14] The Founder of Opus Dei heard and recognised the bells of this church ringing at mid-day on 2 October 1928, just after God had shown him the Work He wanted him to set up, and for which He had been preparing Blessed Josemaría for the past eleven years.

Another place we used to go to in our free time in those Study Weeks was the Prado Museum. There Vicente Rodríguez Casado used to teach us to appreciate art and history. Once or twice Francisco Botella and Fernando Delapuente[15] also showed us the art gallery's treasures. From these three I learnt some notions of the history of art, which enabled me to act as a guide to those who came later to spend a few days in Madrid.

For my part, those intense and varied days were a chapter of marvels. I was one of the youngest. All I had to do was listen and learn and try to reproduce in my own life the mass of teachings that were cascading down upon me.

What with one thing and another there were very many visitors in Jenner that summer, and I'd love to recall all of them. But if I listed them all, readers who had never met them would perhaps find it a trifle lengthy.

Blessed Josemaría's friends

We also saw clergy in Jenner, friends of the Father's who were spending a few days in Madrid, staying in the residence. Among these were Don

---

[15] Fernando Delapuente was born in Santander in 1909. He became an industrial engineer in 1933. In 1929 he had entered the San Fernando School of Fine Arts, but he did not complete his studies until 1939. In 1949 he moved to Rome to help with the decoration of the central building of Opus Dei. He is best known as a painter. He held exhibitions in Paris, New York, Toronto, Madrid, and Barcelona among other places. He died in Madrid in 1975.

Antonio Rodilla, who had been rector of Patriarch Juan de Ribera School in Burjasot, Valencia, and was at that time Vicar General of the Diocese of Valencia; Monsignor Xavier de Lauzurica, Apostolic Administrator of Vitoria; and Monsignor Marcelino Olaechea, Bishop of Pamplona. These and other ecclesiastics would sometimes celebrate Mass in the Oratory and preach to us, encouraging us in our Christian living and praising the priestly work being done by Monsignor Escrivá. I think it was Monsignor Lauzurica, tall and heavily built, who used to make the wooden altar-step groan under him as he moved about while celebrating Mass. Finally, Don Sebastián Cirac, Professor of Greek at the University of Barcelona, used to try and convince us of the excellence of the classical languages, with varying degrees of success. I remember a long conversation in the dining-room about the Latin hyperbaton, reviled by some of us but defended by the learned priest with erudition and simplicity.

The Jenner building

The residence occupied the third floor and the left half of the first floor of 6 Jenner Street. It was a wide, imposing building. Judging by its architecture, it had been built in about 1920. It had a spacious entrance-hall, with a uniformed porter in attendance. There was a very striking lift in the stair-well. It was shaped like one of the old horse-drawn carriages, with mahogany-coloured wood, plenty of glass in the sides and door, and a bench at the back upholstered in red.

The building was shaped like a stubby U, with the horizontal line, the longest, along the street. This shape was apparent on the third floor; the first only included half of it. The horizontal stroke of the U may have been twenty-five or thirty metres long at third floor level. On that floor there were about eighteen or twenty rooms of varying sizes, but most of them fairly large. At the two corners there were rooms measuring three and a half by five metres each: one of them became the Oratory, and the other was a bedroom for four. There were other rooms, such as a small reception room, a multi-purpose room (used for circles of formation, classes, and conversations), a former kitchen which had been converted into Fernando Delapuente's studio, and another used as a toolroom and store-room; two vestibules, the larger of which was used as a sitting-room; and the usual passages and bathrooms. All the other rooms were bedrooms for the residents: about thirteen rooms with one, two, three, or four beds in each.

On the first floor there was a small room which was the Father's bedroom and office; two dining-rooms, one for the residents and one for guests; the kitchen and a small scullery; the room where Grandmother and Aunt Carmen worked; their bedroom; Santiago Escrivá's room; Alvaro del Portillo's; bathrooms; and a small reception room. There were about ten rooms all together.

Activities of Blessed Josemaría

As a matter of fact I noticed very little in this respect. Before I arrived in Jenner, Blessed Josemaría made some journeys to Valladolid, where he had a close friend in Don Daniel Llorente, a priest who later became Bishop of Segovia (he died in 1971) and well known for his outstanding ability in teaching the Faith to children. Don Daniel had previously introduced him to some students. I heard Blessed Josemaría voicing heartfelt praise for Don Daniel. In Valladolid a small group of people had joined Opus Dei not many months before; Teodoro Ruiz, a lawyer, was the first. Then came Juan Antonio Paniagua, at that time a medical student; two brothers, Alberto and Ramón Taboada, the first just finishing his Law degree and the second studying chemistry; Javier Silió, who was about to start his degree in Humanities, and Antonio Moreno, a chemistry student. Shortly afterwards this group was joined by Andrés Vázquez de Prada and Juan Udaondo, both law students, and others. Except for Antonio Moreno, who died prematurely about a year afterwards, the others, after working for a time at their respective professions in Spain, went to begin or reinforce the apostolate of Opus Dei in different countries. I will omit their biographies here so as not to make this account unduly detailed.

On one of his journeys, on 29 June, Blessed Josemaría preached a spiritual retreat to students at Our Lady of Lourdes School, run by the De la Salle brothers. He met two boys from San Sebastián,

Ignacio Echeverría and Jesús Urteaga, who had gone there to take a state examination to convalidate their secondary education, which they needed in order to get in to university. In the course of the retreat he talked to them in depth about the overriding need of seeking God in the ordinary circumstances of their lives. A couple of months later they asked to join the Work.

In the Jenner Residence the Father attended to the spiritual needs of his sons in the Work, all the residents, and a very large number of men of different ages and doing different jobs, who came to him for spiritual direction. As the apostolate had been spreading since the end of the Civil War to cities like Valencia, Barcelona, Valladolid, Saragossa, Bilbao, San Sebastián, and others, Blessed Josemaría had to broaden the government of the Work likewise. He had already appointed an initial Council to help him. Alvaro del Portillo was its Secretary General and Isidoro Zorzano was the Administrator. For the rest, the activity of the Founder of the Work in the residence will be reflected in the different episodes I recount.

Masses in the Oratory

When I arrived in Jenner I was impressed by the way Blessed Josemaría celebrated Mass. I found it deeply moving, and so did everyone, judging by the comments I heard. In the first place, it was the way he celebrated it. He followed the liturgical norms of the Church with great care. Within these rubrics he ensured that the congregation participated in the Holy Sacrifice as actively as possible. His daily Mass was "dialogued", meaning that the responses were given not only by the server, as was usual in churches in those times, but by all of us together, slowly and calmly. This enabled us to be really penetrated by the Eucharistic mystery.

Another factor was that the vestments were both simple and elegant. For example, I had not seen a priest celebrating Mass in a Gothic chasuble before, only in the kind which was usual at that time, the guitar-shaped "Roman" chasubles. In Jenner, with the permission of the Bishop of Madrid, the larger Gothic chasubles were worn, which lent added dignity to the sacred act. The frontal on the altar was changed according to the liturgical colour of the day.

The Oratory was rectangular, with the altar on one of the longer sides, standing a little away from the wall. This made it very much the centre of the room, and the congregation almost surrounded it, so that everyone was close to the altar. Upon it was a square, silver-plated wooden tabernacle, completely covered with a tabernacle veil, which was also of the liturgical colour of the day. On the altar there was a rather large metal crucifix and six metal candle-sticks, with thick candles graded in size, the largest nearest the crucifix; these were lit on feast-days and for Exposition and Benediction of the Blessed Sacrament. On ordinary days two smaller candlesticks were placed between the six big ones. The walls of the Oratory were covered in rather dark hessian, which hung in folds from a wooden frieze running round the walls next to the ceiling. The frieze bore the words from the *Acts of the Apostles* (2:42): *Erant autem perseverantes in doctrina apostolorum, et communicatione fractionis panis, et orationibus* – "And they devoted themselves to the apostles' teaching and fellowship, to the breaking of bread and the prayers."

When Blessed Josemaría was celebrating Mass, with his clear intonation, well-marked pauses, and unconcealed recollection and devotion, being at Mass in Jenner generated deep, sincere piety. I cannot do less than state, after all these years, that those Masses of the Father led me to love the Church's Liturgy and to participate in the Holy Sacrifice with a new attitude. The transcendence of the action being celebrated was something we could see, hear, and touch.

In soldier's trousers

That summer of 1940 in Jenner was a time of shortages of everything; there was only one thing we had a surplus of, and that was military uniforms. After the Civil War those who had completed their time in the ranks were discharged and their uniforms likewise became redundant. But it was not easy to put them to any civilian use. Blessed Josemaría, however, did use them: hidden under his cassock he was able to wear the military trousers belonging to his sons in the

Work; especially some wide ones, gathered below the knee with tapes or elastic. Why spend money on having trousers specially made?

Obviously, people did not know about this economy of the Father's. I found out by chance, perhaps because I didn't have a full-time job. I found out more besides: the trousers he was wearing had belonged to Vicente Rodríguez Casado, who had been a sergeant in the Engineers in the army (I should mention that at that time Vicente did not suffer from the obesity which was a symptom of his illness later on). As priests know, when one walks and genuflects one's trousers rub against one's cassock (and, formerly, against the cloak priests used to wear), and this quickly wears out the trousers at the knee. In this way Blessed Josemaría practised another aspect of the "poverty of the father of a large and poor family", a phrase he coined himself to characterise the Christian sobriety with which members of Opus Dei live. In every poor family, before anything is finally thrown away it is always put to a number of secondary uses.

Years later I heard Blessed Josemaría say that his wearing military trousers in that way was not to be taken as a general guideline or used as a rule of conduct; priests should be properly dressed, whether the clothes can be seen or not. But in those particular circumstances it had been the right way for him to practise poverty.

Fernando Delapuente

Fernando spent many hours working in Jenner, where he lived for part of that summer. Unless I am mistaken he was engineering manager of a sugar factory at Terrer, Saragossa, at the time. But his great love was painting. A former kitchen on the third floor served as his studio, as I have already described. There, among other things, he painted a triptych of the Crucifixion, modelled on a classical painting by the early Flemish artist, Van der Weyden. Fernando jokingly signed his "*Van der Brücke fusilavit Van der Weyden*" (Delapuente shot – slang for copied – Van der Weyden). It turned out splendidly and was used as the altar-piece of the Oratory of Samaniego University Residence in Valencia, which was opened shortly afterwards for the year 1940-41. The Crucifixion triptych is now in one of the small Oratories of the shrine of Our Lady of the Angels at Torreciudad, Huesca.

Given the shortage of industrial goods, Fernando made up most of his paints himself, mixing various substances together, and they often needed stirring constantly to stop them from drying or separating out. Enlisting my help for this job, he used to encourage me with his proverbial cheeriness, explaining how, in the late Middle Ages and the Renaissance, apprentices who later went on to become great painters had started off by mixing paints in the workshop of a good master-painter. But my destiny and talents did not lie there.

The Founder of the Work often used to come into Fernando's studio to encourage him as he worked, to talk over how the paintings were going, and to explain what would be needed for the Oratories and the decoration of the Centres of the Work which were planned for different cities. Fernando's joyous nature was an attraction which drew residents and visitors too, from time to time, to come and look over his painting. Fernando never let them down, always having something funny to tell while he carried on working without a pause.

Offside tally

One day, at the beginning of the third Study Week, which I was participating in, three or four of the newest of us got together in a room which I can remember perfectly. It was not for any specific reason, but just to talk together among ourselves, all of us being very junior in Opus Dei. Carried away by our enthusiasm and also, undoubtedly, our curiosity, we started to count up the number of people in the Work. At that time it was not very difficult, and we managed to make a very approximate list. So we began. Here in Madrid, there is... and in Valencia... and in Valladolid... and in Barcelona... There were not many cities to go through. We ended up with a figure that must have been very close to the truth. And, feeling we had ascertained something of interest, "there being no further business to discuss, the meeting was closed".

A few days later the Founder of the Work gave a formative talk on personal and collective humility. He told us that in order to maintain personal humility, which everyone individually needs to make an effort to practise as the basis for any growth in Christian living, God has disposed that in Opus Dei we should make the effort to practise collective humility as well, to avoid the danger of being collectively proud. As he explained very clearly: "If John and Peter and Andrew, taken individually, are supposed to be humble, I cannot understand why together they can have the right to be as proud as peacocks."[16] He continued his explanation for some time, showing how important he considered this virtue to be in the spirit of the Work.

The lesson of that talk had been set out very clearly in a letter of his dated 9 January 1932. In it he said, "The theological virtue of hope gives us such a great appreciation for the reward our Father God has promised us, that we don't wish to risk losing it through a lack of collective humility. We don't wish to have applied to us, for having sought the applause of men, those words of our Lord: *Amen, dico vobis, receperunt mercedem suam:* truly, I say to you, they have their reward (Matt 6:16). How sad it would be!" And he wound up by applying this in practice. Not in

---

[16] The words quoted are taken from a letter from Blessed Josemaría dated 31 May 1954. But when I read them I remembered that these words were very similar, almost identical, to what he had said to us in 1940.

these exact words, but very nearly, he told us, "That is why we do not publish statistics of our projects, or the number of members, or the fruits obtained in our apostolates, when these would only serve to satisfy people's curiosity or foster a sense of self-satisfaction. We are not interested in statistics. We don't go around counting how many of us there are. There are as many of us as our Lord wants."[17]

The talk given by the Founder of Opus Dei made me blush inside. Obviously, what we had done was silly. I wondered whether our Father had explained that important aspect of the virtue of humility because of our calculations a few days earlier, or whether it was just a coincidence. I never tried to find out, nor did I discuss it with any of the newcomers who had talked together on that occasion. The whole question was quite clear, and the only thing that mattered was to alter my behaviour: that episode, and many others besides, was left permanently engraved on my memory.

The silent sowing of prayer, penance, and sufferings of Blessed Josemaría, particularly intensely during the war years when his apostolic work was so severely restricted by circumstances, had borne a very abundant harvest. "The plants were hidden under the snow. And the farmer who owned the land remarked with satisfaction, 'Now they're growing on the inside'.

---

[17] A paragraph from a letter dated 31 May 1954 filled in further aspects of what he told us in Jenner: "If we were to contract this weakness we would immediately begin to lose our collective humility and would be in danger of acquiring an '*esprit de corps*' which is divisive and therefore not very ecumenical."

I thought of you, of your forced inactivity... Tell me, are you too growing 'on the inside'?"[18]

Obviously, Opus Dei's collective humility does not mean that it fails to pass on to the Holy See all the information which is needed for the governance of the universal Church. Similarly, the Prelature of Opus Dei publishes a twice-yearly information booklet in Rome, called *Romana*. This, naturally, is no lack of collective humility; it is simply abiding within the sphere of the law and government of our Mother the Church. Once these reckonings have been made and this information given, neither of which are secret, they are passed on to the press and other public information services, when requested. For its part, the Holy See publishes the number of faithful in the Prelature every year in the *Annuario Pontificio*, as it does for the other institutions of the Catholic Church.

"To the barricades!"

On one of the last days of the Work Week I went to see Blessed Josemaría, who received us on that occasion in the room belonging to the director of the residence. I told him freely about the state of my soul and the impressions made on me by those days. From the start it had been a natural custom for the members of Opus Dei to talk with the Founder simply and frankly about the progress of their souls, their resolutions, the joys and difficulties that arose in their inner and external life, and so on. It was the spiritual

---

[18] Blessed Josemaría Escrivá, *The Way*, 294.

guidance that was natural in the specific circumstances of our desire to seek holiness in the fulfilment of our duties as ordinary citizens and Christians. The Father gave me some guidance on the particular points I had spoken of and encouraged me in a friendly and demanding way.

When we ended our conversation he said, "To the barricades!" His meaning was perfectly clear to me in the general context of those times and the things I had just been talking about. It was a stimulus for my personal ascetical struggle, phrased in the terminology of the times, little more than a year since the end of the Civil War, when military-style language was still very current. It suggested firmness in my resolutions and an outlook of courage and optimism. The fact that I have never forgotten this farewell shows the stimulating effect it had on me.

My first day of recollection

I am not sure if it was during the September Work Week or slightly earlier, in August, that I made my first ever day of recollection. But I do remember the two meditations the Father preached to us that day. The first was on the universal call to holiness with specific applications to the demands God was making on us, the people there. He spoke with such force, conviction, and authority that for the first time I saw clearly that holiness, taken in its strict sense, was not some utopian dream but an attainable goal, with the help of God's grace and the use of the means for sanctification.

Like many Christians, I had previously imagined holiness as a distant, inaccessible ideal, something granted by God to those phenomena whom we call the saints – admirable people, but strange, and impossible to imitate in practice. It is true that from my first contacts with Opus Dei, and as an effect of reading *The Way* from Christmas 1939 onwards, the task of Christian sanctification had sunk more and more into me. But up until that meditation from our Founder I do not remember having felt such an ardent, almost heart-shaking desire for it, nor having experienced the possibility, or rather the personal need, of aspiring to that holiness without any half-measures. I did not know how to channel the impulses aroused so forcefully by his words, into specific resolutions; but one thing was quite clear: no other prospect existed than that of becoming holy, through the effort to fulfil the ordinary duties of every day. And, finally, it was clear that this task, though a hard one in itself, was possible, since God wanted it and granted his graces for the struggle to achieve it.

I had reached this point when we went back into the Oratory for the second meditation. It was all about sanctification through daily work. In the same way as before, we heard about the need to make good use of our time, to offer to our Lord all the effort we made in studying, doing it in God's presence, and considering it not as self-affirmation but as a means of sanctification and apostolate, as a way of strengthening our characters and as a responsibility we had

Dolores Albás y Blanc (1877-1941), mother of Blessed Josemaría Escrivá. From a painting by Fernando Bayo.

Rome, 1956: Carmen Escrivá de Balaguer, (1899-1957) sister of Blessed Josemaría Escrivá.

Torrevieja, July 1951: José María's parents at his first Mass. In the centre is the parish priest of Torrevieja.

Fr José María Casciaro, now a biblical scholar.

towards God and other people.

It was the first time I had done a day of recollection and I didn't know the right way to do it. I didn't know that it was a good idea to reflect and meditate on the themes and make the relevant resolutions, so as to put them into practice later on in normal life. So when the meditation ended I went back to my room, picked out a book, and sat down in the hall of the residence for some intense study. After a while, someone took me aside and explained how to do a day of recollection, giving me to understand that as a consequence I should leave studying the textbook for later.

I have just described, with conscious simplicity and ingenuity, the first impressions made on me by the Father's preaching. The testimony of many other people agrees with mine as they express, each in their own way, the effects of Blessed Josemaría's words: at once penetrating, encouraging, friendly, and demanding. I found it very different in form and content from the few religious sermons I had heard in my life. Perhaps my experience in that sphere was limited, but the Father's preaching was an altogether new thing for me.

There is still something else I wish to add. When, many years later, I read the homily "Towards Holiness" in the book *Friends of God*, I immediately remembered that first meditation in Jenner Residence. They were both on the same theme and approximately along the same lines, although the spoken language of the meditation was backed up by the expressive force of his living word, his warm tones and his gestures, which obviously cannot be conveyed by a printed text. From all of this I draw further considerations now, such as, for example, Blessed Josemaría's extraordinary degree of spiritual maturity while still young, but I am not going to go into these at length, in accordance with my decision to limit myself in this book to the memories of what I felt in those years of my youth.

Chapter Six

Family atmosphere
(Jenner, Summer 1940 (cont.))

Grandmother and Aunt Carmen

When I arrived in Jenner Street, having brought my school year to a successful conclusion, I did not have any more studying to do until the following October. This relative freedom from schoolwork gave me the opportunity to spend a lot of time with Doña Dolores and Carmen Escrivá, who were looking after the domestic work in the residence. The director of the residence gave me two responsibilities which facilitated this still further: repairs and looking after the Oratory.

The first job took up most of my time. Quite often, under the guidance of Doña Dolores and Aunt Carmen, I used to do small repairs on the kitchen utensils or cleaning things, which in those times were less complex and technical than they are now, since electrical equipment scarcely existed.

One thing I should make clear: in Jenner I found that the older people in the Work called Doña Dolores "Grandmother" and used the familiar *"tu"* with her and Aunt Carmen.[†] The reason for this was that in most of Spain, within the family, people normally use *tu*, even with their grandparents. And "the Work is a family, a big one, with supernatural ties", as our Founder often described it. When the older people referred to them in their absence they called them "Grandmother", and "Aunt Carmen" or simply "Carmen". I found it quite difficult to use *tu* when speaking to Grandmother, or to call her by that name. I soon got used to saying "Grandmother", but never *tu*, and when I spoke to her I used to employ roundabout forms to avoid saying either *usted* or *tu*. I do not know how I managed. I remember thinking several times that I could ask Alvaro del Portillo about it, since I used to talk to him about my personal concerns. But when I was actually talking with him there was always something else that seemed more important and I forgot to ask him about that particular matter. So I carried on having to deal with the problem each time it came up, as I have said.

Going back to my responsibility for maintenance in Jenner Residence, I remember that on one occasion I had to install a large meat-mincer on the marble kitchen table. I had to make four good-sized holes in the marble so that the bolts attached to the mincer could fit through them and be fixed in place with butterfly-nuts. I did not have any kind of drill, either

---

[†] Translator's note: Like most European languages, Spanish has both a familiar and a polite form of "you". The familiar form of "you" in the singular is *tu*, and the polite form is *usted*.

mechanical or electric. I made the holes with a large screwdriver and a hammer, striking gently with one hand and turning the screwdriver with the other. Obviously it was a slow and tricky job, and it must have taken me more than one day. From time to time Grandmother and Aunt Carmen came to see how the job was coming on, perhaps a little sceptically to begin with but growing more hopeful as the holes got deeper and the rest of marble remained undamaged. They encouraged me in my patient task. In the end the marble was duly drilled through and the mincing-machine fixed firmly in place.

"Mother, you're going to spoil him on me"

As a reward for this operation, Grandmother gave me an enormous sweet, one of the kind known as "Calatayud paving-stones", which I had never seen before. As a matter of fact they both used to look out for opportunities to make me eat a bit extra, because they were worried by my thinness at that time. I heard Grandmother say more than once, "That boy is very thin". We had gone into the small room where Grandmother and Aunt Carmen used to spend the afternoon. It was about five o'clock when she gave me the sweet. I put it in my mouth, intending to bite off a bit, but realised it was impossible to do so because it was so big, and I was left with the whole "paving-stone" in my mouth.

At that very moment Blessed Josemaría came in and said something to me. My mouth was completely full of the sweet and when I tried to answer, all I could manage were some inarticulate noises. The Father, surprised, asked, "What's the matter with him?" Grandmother explained the situation. The Father immediately turned towards the door, clearly not wanting to go any further into the matter, and said, smiling, "Mother, you're going to spoil him on me." And he went away.

The episode has no particular significance. It touches on the spheres of a well-disciplined upbringing and Christian sobriety: it is not advisable to eat between meals. Anyway, it shows the simple, natural homeliness of family life in the Work.

Conversations in Grandmother's room

In Jenner there was much coming and going in the summer of 1940. Those who came for the Study Weeks, and people who came to Madrid to spend even a few days with the Father, were avid to know about everything: people, news about the Work, places where the Founder had developed his apostolate from its beginnings, and so on. As well as more strictly spiritual care, these very legitimate wishes were also attended to. Our rendezvous for setting out to show them round the different places soon came to be, quite naturally, the small room where Grandmother and Aunt Carmen usually spent most of the afternoon mending clothes, table-cloths, sheets, and so on, and sewing the linen cloths used for Holy Mass.

While we were waiting for each other in Grandmother's room, we frequently used to start lively conversations with her and Aunt Carmen. Without ceasing to work for a moment, they returned wise, prudent answers to the questions, sometimes rather indiscreet ones, which we rained down on them, about the Father's childhood, the difficulties of the war years, and many other things besides. They never got into difficulties: they would give intelligent answers to some questions and gracefully side-step others.

The love they felt for all of us, even the first time they met someone, was clear to see. It was as though they had always known us. As well as the teachings of our Father, there can be no doubt that the example they both set was a major factor in shaping the family atmosphere of the Work at a time of great growth. Grandmother and Aunt Carmen were affectionate without being affected, effortlessly friendly, understanding towards our youthful importunity, very human and very supernatural at the same time, and extremely generous in their self-giving to everyone.

To give one example of those gatherings in Grandmother's room, one day Amadeo de Fuenmayor put his head round the door. He was doing his military service in Vicálvaro, near Madrid. He was on leave for the weekend and had come in his soldier's uniform, leggings buttoned up tightly round his calves, looking very thin, tanned by drilling for hours under the Castillian summer sunshine, and wearing the forage-cap which was standard issue in those days. The gesture he made as he came into the room was a poem in itself, humorously expressive of his joy. Undoubtedly he was thinking how much his attire was going to amuse Grandmother and Aunt Carmen. It did. It delighted them and really made them laugh. He related his adventures in the barracks and we – I was there, of course – had a marvellous time.

Many of the people who turned up unexpectedly were introduced, or introduced themselves, to Grandmother and Aunt Carmen. And the conversation was enlivened with news about their respective towns, their studies, and the little incidents of their eventful journeys to Madrid at a time when the means of transport were so precarious.

A large and poor family

I have already mentioned that this was a phrase which Blessed Josemaría sometimes used to describe the Work. In the summer of 1940 I had a chance to see one of its manifestations for myself. In the hours when Grandmother and Aunt Carmen were working I observed how they put everything to good use, applying skill, ingenuity, and effort. For example, sheets usually get worn thin and torn in the middle much sooner than at the sides. There was no question of buying new ones. In a large and poor family everything is used up. Out of several sheets which had worn thin, Grandmother and Aunt Carmen would make one almost new one. They patched the thinnest part with a piece of material in good condition, making a square or rectangle to place over the centre. But the stitches were done so perfectly that they could not be felt, and hardly even seen.

Something that took up a lot of their time was mending shirts. They would make new cuffs and collars to replace worn-out ones, cutting material from the shirt-tail and replacing it with material that matched as closely as possible (in those days nobody ever wore their shirts outside their trousers). There was also the task of darning socks; in the days before synthetic fibres, heels and toes soon wreaked havoc in socks. The wooden egg was an object which Grandmother and Aunt Carmen made constant use of to mend them.

Yet another task was the making and upkeep of vestments and altar-linen: they were always carefully mended, well ironed, and, when necessary, starched. I can imagine, though only in the broadest terms, how much the women in the Work must have learnt about all these tasks, and the exquisite care to take of them, from Grandmother and Aunt Carmen. A family which is poor, but hard-working and clean, finds ways to make use of things that a rich family would throw away without thinking twice about it. This careful concern to repair things and make them last has been, from the start, a prominent aspect of the way people in Opus Dei practise poverty: a Christian virtue which, if it goes together with clean, neat clothes, does not attract attention in a way that is showy, or unpleasant for other people.

Isidoro Zorzano

In Jenner I found Isidoro. He was one of the few people I had met before, on that day at the beginning of May 1939 in the rector's house at the St Elizabeth Foundation. His room was next to the Oratory and was connected to it by a double door; it served as the secretary's room for the residence, the economic administration office for the Work, a bedroom, and the place where the vessels and other objects for the Oratory, and the priest's liturgical vestments, were kept. There was no room for anything else. Cushions disguised the bed to some extent, making it look like a divan.

During those months, presumably because of the special summer timetable, Isidoro used to go in to work very early, at eight o'clock in the morning, I seem to remember. His office was in the Development Office of the RENFE, near the Delicias railway station, at that time an area on the outskirts of Madrid, which meant a long journey. To arrive on time he had to get up at about five o'clock, summertime (which would be four or even three o'clock by the sun), since he had several things to do. Shaving was particularly difficult for Isidoro; the hair on his chin was very tough and he had extremely delicate skin, and it was made worse by the poor quality of the "Toledo" brand razor-blades, a national brand which used the type of steel then available. He sharpened the blade every day, using a plain glass which he first wetted with water; otherwise he would have needed a new blade every time he shaved. He had to leave his room perfectly tidy so that it could be used afterwards as a sacristy and a confessional. He did half an hour of mental prayer and went to a church to hear Mass; at that time, Mass was celebrated in the mornings only.

One of Isidoro's characteristics was his passion for tidiness. I was in charge of the Oratory, and every morning I went to his room a little before the beginning of the prayer to finalize the preparation of the vestments for Mass in the residence. There was not a single day on which he failed to leave his room absolutely ready, clean, and aired. I do not remember ever having heard him make the slightest mention of the difficulties involved in getting up so very early, which, undoubtedly, he offered to God in a joyful spirit of penance and mortification.

He came home from work after three in the afternoon. He had a quick lunch and started dealing with the economic administration of the Work and the residence, on which he worked together with Grandmother and Aunt Carmen. He had put together a card-index calculating the cost of the different meals per head: so many grams of rice, or lentils, or whatever it was, per resident, worked out at so much per meal. In Spain after the Civil War a period of food shortages had begun, and it was very difficult to provide "healthy, plentiful food" for the residents in Jenner. Other domestic supplies were also unobtainable, or of poor quality, since the after-effects of the Spanish

Civil War were made still worse by the Second World War: some things could not be imported. Those were the times which Juan Jiménez Vargas later referred to humorously as "the times before under-development". Grandmother, Aunt Carmen, and Isidoro worked diligently and skilfully to overcome these shortages with style.

There are certain things about Isidoro which I remember particularly. Among these are some of the expressions he used, which showed the care he took to practise detachment even in the smallest details. For example, he always avoided saying that anything was his. He did this in different ways, sometimes saying "the pen I use" so as not to say "my pen". Or "the room where I sleep", instead of "my room", and so on. I have a feeling he never once got this wrong, which means it was a habit he had acquired by dint of continual effort.

Walks with "Uncle Isidoro"

One day, when I had been living in Jenner Street for about a week, I was in a passage, preparing to hang a large china plate on the wall as part of the decoration. It must have been a little after four in the afternoon. The Father went by, stopped, and asked me, "Pepe, when do you go out?" He probably thought I was looking a little pale. I had to stop and think before I answered: some days I used to go to a nearby ironmonger's, at the Chamberí junction, to stock up with what I needed for my work: nails, screws, insulating-tape, switches, light-bulbs, etc. The Father did not wait. Without further delay he said something like, "You should go out every day to get some fresh air and have a walk. But not at this time of day" – the waves of heat characteristic of Madrid at the beginning of August were making themselves felt in their full strength – "but in the late afternoon, when the sun isn't so hot." He added a few more sentences which I do not remember, and went away.

A few minutes later Isidoro came up and invited me to go for a walk with him every day in the late afternoon, when the sun was not so hot. His words were very similar to those the Father had used. There was no doubt as to what had happened: Blessed Josemaría had found it would be a good thing for Isidoro to do the same. And so we began to do what had been suggested.

We used to have a fairly short walk. We would arrange a time to meet in Grandmother's room. Naturally, I used to get there a few minutes early and wait. Every day, Isidoro took me to one or other of the places where the Father had begun his apostolate with young men: the *El Sotanillo* café, the site of the DYA Academy, Ferraz Street, and so on. He would explain the history of the place we were going to and always managed to pass on some of our Founder's teachings in the course of our conversations. After a short walk we used to get home, a little before the evening meal.

One day, when I arrived at our usual meeting-place, Grandmother said, laughing, "Your Uncle Isidoro came to say that he'll be a bit late today because an unexpected job has come up; but you're to wait for him, because you'll go out together no matter what happens."

And we both laughed. It was true: it was like an uncle going for walks with his nephew, because at thirty-eight Isidoro was more than twice my age.

"Make the whole day into a Mass"

Those walks with "Uncle Isidoro" must have gone on for about ten days, because, as I shall relate, other circumstances stopped them. During them Isidoro explained a lot of things about the Work to me. One afternoon, as we were walking through the streets of Madrid, he explained to me what the Father taught about the Holy Mass as the centre and root of the interior life. Isidoro talked to me about how to make the whole day hinge around the Eucharist, how to "make the whole day into a Mass", in Blessed Josemaría's words. For me these explanations from Isidoro were discoveries, given the few months I had been in the Work. In the times that followed I was to hear repeatedly and directly from the Father's lips the same explanations as I had previously heard from Isidoro, and which can be summed up in the words he wrote in *The Forge*, 69: "Keep struggling, so that the Holy Sacrifice of the Altar really becomes the centre and the root of your interior life, and so your whole day will turn into an act of worship: an extension of the Mass you have attended and a preparation for the next. This will then overflow into aspirations, visits to the Blessed Sacrament and the offering up of your professional work and your family life."[1]

Some twenty-five years later, the Second Vatican Council taught authoritatively that "the liturgy is the summit towards which the activity of the Church is directed; it is also the fount from which all her power flows,"[2] and also that "the eucharistic celebration is the centre of the assembly of the faithful... hence priests teach the faithful to offer the divine victim to God the Father in the sacrifice of the Mass and with the victim to make an offering of their whole life."[3] When I read these and other statements of the Second Vatican Council I could not help remembering the teachings I had heard from our beloved Founder's lips more than twenty years before.

"If we're faithful, we'll soon be going abroad"

On another day, as we were strolling along a broad pavement in front of Nuevos Ministerios, Isidoro told me, "The Father has said that if we're faithful, we'll soon be going abroad".

Today this statement may seem trivial, because, among other things, it is now common for students to travel abroad without any difficulty. But if we go back to those times, it opened up a totally new

---

[1] And which led him to conclude in *The Way*, 533: "That is why I must love the Mass so much! (*Our* Mass, Jesus.)"
[2] Constitution *Sacrosanctum Concilium*, 10.
[3] Decree *Presbyterorum Ordinis*, 5.

horizon. Because of the Second World War it was very difficult to obtain visas; you had to satisfy endless questions and wait for a long time, perhaps months; and the matter was even more difficult if you were applying for a residence permit. Similarly, it was very hard work to obtain an exit visa if the applicant was of military age, as was the case for most of those of the Work. But the Father was not held back by difficulties. Obviously the news that Isidoro had just given me was a tremendous stimulus. It was not just a question of expansion into the different regions of Spain, but of beginning to put into practice the universal dimension of Opus Dei, which had been one of its essential features from its inception.

I have often recalled those words which Isidoro passed on from the Father. One of the occasions, not too long ago, was an evening in August 1990, on the terrace of the Notre Dame guest-house for pilgrims in Jerusalem. A group composed of seven members of Opus Dei had had dinner and were sitting talking together in tranquillity, although the Gulf War had just broken out with the invasion of Kuwait by Iraqi troops. The six people there were: Alberto Steinvorth, born in Costa Rica of German parents; Francisco Varo, from Cordoba, Spain; Gervais Kpan, from Côte d'Ivoire; Barry Cole, English; Miguel Angel Tábet, a Venezuelan whose parents were Lebanese; and myself. Albert and Barry had been living in Jerusalem for a year, having started the apostolate of the Work there. The rest of us were spending a few months there for the

Madrid, March 1935: Blessed Josemaría with students attending activities at Ferraz.

Madrid: The house at 14, Diego de León Street.

Rome, April 1968: Blessed Josemaría with Fr Alvaro del Portillo and Fr Javier Echevarría.

Rome, May 1992: Fr Pedro Casciaro in St Peter's Square, at the beatification of Josemaría Escrivá.

purposes of our study and research. At a given moment, looking at the variety of the people gathered there, there came to my memory the words, "If we're faithful, we'll soon be going abroad". And once again I was filled with faith in our Founder's words, and with gratitude to God for having called me to the splendid adventure of the Work in my earliest youth.

Another of these times was experienced by thousands of people on 17 May 1992, at the beatification of Monsignor Josemaría Escrivá by Pope John Paul II in St Peter's Square, in Rome, and at the concelebrated Mass of thanksgiving the following day, presided over by Monsignor Alvaro del Portillo, in the same place. On both occasions, a huge crowd of people from very many countries and of every sort were there as a tangible result of the words Isidoro Zorzano had passed on to me from the Founder of the Work in summer 1940. For those of us who had come to Opus Dei when it was small, to see it having grown so much was very moving indeed.

Intensive study

Blessed Josemaría's care for all his children was constant. I have just mentioned his concern for our health and even, in some cases, for the way we looked, with reference to his suggestion about going for walks. Now I will go on to talk about my studies.

We had been going for walks for barely ten days when Isidoro and Paco Botella or Vicente Rodríguez Casado, I don't remember which, spoke to me of the possibility of bringing forward the seventh year of my secondary schooling and taking the fearful state examination, all in the September examination period. There was only a month till the examinations. For various reasons, I have no doubt that the idea originated from the Father, although they did not say this to me in so many words. It seemed a very good idea to me and I was grateful and even enthusiastic about it, although it would mean a considerable effort. They helped me to draw up an application to the National Education Ministry, which we sent in straight away.

Isidoro, Paco and Vicente gave me some tests to do. The results showed that I had a good grounding in the arts subjects but some gaps in the sciences. So an intense period of preparation began for the September examinations, which were just around the corner. Isidoro was my science teacher. Every day, after his late lunch, we would go to a small room which had a blackboard, and he would explain the main topics of mathematics, physics and chemistry which were included in the programmes I was to be examined on. The other part of the session consisted of me explaining those same topics to him in my turn. And this was the trying part for Isidoro. I have already mentioned how he was a little short of sleep because he had to get up so early. To this was added the time of day, the heat of the Madrid summer, and finally the boring tones of my explanations. Isidoro was often overcome by sleep. I felt too sorry for him to interrupt his brief nap, until, after a very few minutes, he would rouse himself and scold me for not having woken him. I apologised and we went on with our work, without any further interruptions, until the agreed time. This scene did not take place every day, but certainly on several. I need not stress how much effort and sacrifice must have been involved for Isidoro in giving me those classes in the midst of all the other things he had to do.

Obviously, I spent the rest of the day studying those science subjects and working on my own on the arts subjects, with sporadic assessment by Vicente Rodríguez Casado. Things went on in this way for about three weeks, until I received the reply from the Ministry: the request was rejected because I had already been credited with the three years of the war, in the special examinations held to revalidate the years I had studied in the "Red Zone", and therefore there were no grounds for granting my application.

Although the Ministry was right, we (and especially the Father, I realised from people's comments when the reply came) had been really keen on the idea of my starting university the very next year. But it was not going to be possible. They cheered me up, and for a few days I stopped giving priority to my books and returned to the pincers, hammer and pliers. There was still most of September left before the school year began again.

Alvaro del Portillo and Juan Jiménez Vargas

I saw a lot of Alvaro that summer. We used to

meet for a conversation every week, in which I told him about my plans, resolutions, difficulties, and so on. He gave me advice which was always specific and practical about how to improve in my spiritual life and my behaviour in general.[4] Naturally he explained aspects of the spirit of the Work to me, with continual references to what the Founder had said and written, quoting his teachings word for word unhesitatingly, with a prodigious memory which impressed me from the start. His help was invaluable in those first months of my life in Opus Dei. Alvaro was always understanding and at the same time friendly and demanding: he combined theory with practical help, giving me both reasons for feeling encouraged and help to pinpoint the aspects I needed to make the effort to improve on or correct.

He also wanted to ensure that I was in good health: one day he invited me out to do some sport, namely to go rowing on the lake in Retiro Park. There was a popular facility offered by the State Department of Education and Recreation, which hired out

---

[4] The Bible recommends: "Stay constantly with a godly person whom you know to be a keeper of the commandments, whose soul is in accord with your soul, and who will grieve with you if you fail" (Sir 37:12). In line with the experience of the people of God in the Old Testament, there was born in Opus Dei quite spontaneously, fulfilling an obvious need, the custom of the first members opening their heart to the Founder. "I didn't have a teacher," Blessed Josemaría wrote later, "and it was the Holy Spirit who taught me." And, concerning this, Alvaro del Portillo recalls, "The first people, absolutely freely, got into the habit of telling the Father about all their concerns, opening their consciences wide to him, outside confession; and, when the Father was not there, or when the apostolate began to grow, our first brothers would go to the Director, with the same openness of spirit."

rowing-boats or fishing-boats by the hour at a very low price – a political price. I liked the proposal, and we hired a two-oared boat. Having grown up in Torrevieja, a port, I considered myself an expert oarsman. But I got a surprise: Alvaro rowed not only more strongly – he was much more robust than I was – but also very skilfully. The result, which I had not expected, was that our course was a curve instead of a straight line: he was on the outside of the curve and I was on the inside. Anyway, the physical exercise and the conversation with Alvaro were very stimulating.

Because of this I put my name down for rowing on other occasions, organised by Juan Jiménez Vargas. We did not go very many times, but it was highly enjoyable. It was usually Juan, some of the visitors, and other residents from Jenner. We would hire a rowing-boat for five: four rowers and the cox. Juan was a fiend for rowing: so the two best rowers had to sit on the other side, because he pulled harder than anyone else. What is more, he was tireless. He kept going for the whole hour without slackening the pace, and when anyone, not unnaturally, showed signs of tiring, he encouraged them to keep up the effort with different arguments: "it was good for the health to push one's muscles and heart to the limit" (Juan specialised in human physiology); and on the other hand it would actually be "a fault against Christian poverty to waste the few minutes" that remained until our time was up. With encouragement of that sort the hour's rowing was used to the full.

Chapter Seven

Expansion from Jenner
(Autumn 1940)

Train journeys to the provinces

With the Father and the people who were joining the Work, it would be true to say that the residence at 6 Jenner Street was a reservoir of spiritual energy which had been building up since the summer of 1939. From it they made frequent journeys to the main cities of Spain to spread the apostolate. They used to go at weekends: some of the members of the Work would leave Madrid by the Saturday night trains. They spent Sunday in their chosen city and came back that same night, to get to work or to class on Monday morning. Blessed Josemaría Escrivá often made quick journeys of this kind too. I have mentioned one or two of them in previous chapters. All such days were practically heroic, since besides spending two nights on a train, usually third-class, there was also the fact that railway journeys in those times were highly uncomfortable experiences. The old coal-burning engines were simply machines for producing smoke and cinders, and the carriages, which had been through the destruction of the Spanish Civil War, were in a sorry state.

There was every excuse for such conditions, since the railways had been a military target for both armies during the three years of the war. Moreover, the outbreak of the Second World War made it impossible to import necessary materials from abroad. Everything had to be supplied by the newly-starting national manufacturing or maintenance industries, and the coal produced was of poor quality. Trains would stop frequently at any point in the journey so that the engine boilers could get up steam for the next ascent. But one thing is clear about the history of Opus Dei in those years: if those journeys had not been made in spite of the extreme discomfort involved, the expansion of the Work would have been seriously held up, because it was quite a long time before travelling conditions achieved any degree of comfort.

Those discomforts were accepted with joy, and nobody gave them the slightest importance. They formed part of the collection of prayer, sacrifices, and penances mustered in support of the apostolic activity so that God would grant his graces. The Civil War being still recent in people's minds, and war vocabulary still current, we used to call the supernatural helps which were applied before undertaking those apostolic ventures, "artillery bombardment" (the expression was taken from the normal procedures of combat troops before the infantry attacked a position).

It occurs to me that the above-mentioned build-up of spiritual energies may be compared to the hypothetical concentration of mass and initial energy which, according to the Big Bang theory, started the whole universe expanding. Besides the journeys to cities in the provinces during the second half of 1939 and the whole of the academic year 1939-40, in the summer of 1940 three more Centres of the Work were opened by people who had been living in Jenner Street: in Valencia, the Samaniego Residence, a university hall; in Madrid, in September, the Centre at 15 Martínez Campos Street, for apostolate with people who had finished their studies; and in October, the house in Diego de León Street, at the corner with Lagasca Street.

Samaniego Residence in Valencia

Since the summer of 1939 the apostolate in Valencia had been very intense. Blessed Josemaría had preached several spiritual retreats and had spoken in depth with plenty of young working men and students about the need to lead an intense Christian life. In this way there already existed a good group of people who had asked for admission to the Work: José Manuel Casas,[1] José Orlandis,[2] Amadeo

---

[1] José Manuel Casas Torres was born in 1916. He was one of the first people to join Opus Dei in Valencia at the end of the Spanish Civil War. As Professor of Geography at the University of Saragossa, he carried out significant research into the Pyrenees region and trained many disciples in his branch of learning.

[2] Don José Orlandis Rovira, a lawyer, was born in Palma de Mallorca in 1918. In 1942 he obtained the chair of History of Law at the

de Fuenmayor, Justo Martí, Ismael and Florencio Sánchez Bella, Salvador Moret, Federico Suárez, and probably others, whom I cannot remember for the simple reason that I did not live there myself.

And more students kept coming, who also asked to be admitted to Opus Dei very soon, like Emilio Palafox, Vicente Garín, Angel López Amo, Manuel Botas, and others.

The apostolic fruits, then, were abundant. The Father had started work on opening a hall of residence for university students in Valencia back in 1936. But the project had been interrupted by the Civil War, and he now saw the opportunity and decided to widen the scope of the Christian formational activities held there.

They wanted something to take over from the little mezzanine apartment known as *El Cubil* [3] at 9 Samaniego Street.[4]

Very close by, at number 16 of the same street, they found and rented a fairly large old house. It was a somewhat curious structure, with rooms of very different sizes, some of them with very high ceilings. For example, in the middle of the room which was

---

University of Murcia, and then at the University of Saragossa. He lived in Rome for most of the Second World War, pursuing his studies. He was ordained a priest in 1949. Later he became a lecturer and Dean of the Faculty of Canon Law at the University of Navarre, and then director of the Institute of the History of the Church at the same university. He is a prolific research worker on the History of Law and of the Church. He has also published several spiritual books.

[3] "The Den"

[4] *El Cubil* had opened in July 1939.

fitted out as a sitting-room, there was a real well with a parapet and water. I suppose that it had originally been a patio. Anyway, the new house was set up as a small hall of residence for students, where apostolate could be done as it had been in the Ferraz Street residence before the Civil War and in Jenner from 1939 onwards.

Late in the summer of 1940 Pedro, with Amadeo, who had finished his military service, moved to Valencia to set up the residence in Samaniego Street and work as Director and Sub-director respectively. The idea was that it should open in October, and it did.

Pedro and Amadeo had worked flat out with the others in Valencia to set up the residence. Of course they had very few means of any kind at their disposal, except supernatural ones. Since the women of the Work were not yet able to take on the domestic work, Pedro appealed to my former nurse, Virginia, who had stayed on in our parents' house until the end of the Civil War. She was about fifty, so she was quite experienced, and was all the more to be relied on because of her affection for our family and her piety.

Portraits of my great-grandparents

Meanwhile, our grandfather Julio, undoubtedly wishing to reward my brother for his good offices during the Civil War, had made him a present of two portraits of his own parents, large, good-quality paintings, done in oils in about 1870, with contemporary frames. Our great-grandfather was also called Pedro Casciaro and was the original Englishman, who had been born in Gibraltar and educated in London. Not having anything else for the decoration of Samaniego Residence, Pedro hung them in the reception room there. They went nicely with the furniture in the room and solved the problem of how to fill the huge blank space of the very high walls.

Some months later Don Julio made a journey to Valencia and went to see Pedro. He was shown into the reception room while someone went to find Pedro. And, of course, he found himself face to face with the portraits of his parents. Grandfather and grandson had a very entertaining chat there. Don Julio, who had quite a sense of humour, said that he had almost felt as if he were in his own house. He enjoyed the whole affair. The portraits stayed in that room for some time: I saw them there myself years afterwards. What I do not know is what the residents said about the portraits of the great-grandparents of the Director of the residence.

The Martínez Campos Centre

I do not know when the Father decided to open a new Centre in Madrid to carry on the apostolate he had been doing for years with young working men. But in September 1940 some of the residents from Jenner Street moved to a fairly large flat at 15 Martínez Campos Street (I think it is now number 13). I remember that the people who moved there were Juan Jiménez, Ricardo Fernández Vallespín, Francisco Botella, Vicente Rodríguez Casado, José Luis Múzquiz, and one or two more, including Alfredo Carrato, who was not in the Work. Some of them had finished their studies a few years before; others were just starting them, or were putting the final touches to their doctoral theses. With some of the younger people from Jenner Street, I went there several times to help in setting up the house and to lend a hand in correcting copies of theses.

Blessed Josemaría went there often. He took a direct interest in the installation of the house. I often saw Alvaro del Portillo and José Luis Múzquiz with him. The Centre quickly began to fulfill its intended purpose, and young working men went there who had formerly gone to the DYA Academy or the residences in Ferraz Street and Jenner Street. The Father began to see them there. A sign was put up on the door of the flat which said "Society for Intellectual Co-operation (SOCOIN)", which was the name it had been registered under.

Months afterwards, at the end of May 1941, in the magazine *Qué Pasa*,[5] a short article appeared, enclosed in a box. Its content was more or less as follows: "Beware of the new heretics: Socoinites, Saint-Michaels..." and a few more short sentences enlarging confusedly on the previous ones. As far as I know this was the first time the apostolate of the Work had been mentioned in the press. The tone was

---

[5] *"What's Happening"*

insulting. The founder of the magazine, Joaquín Pérez Madrigal, one of the radicals known as "Wild Boars" because of their aggressiveness during the time of the Second Spanish Republic, had gone over to the extreme right wing when the Civil War was over. This event was one of a series of adversities the Founder of Opus Dei endured after the Civil War, which made him suffer greatly and which he underwent peacefully, with Christian charity and a supernatural outlook.

Then, as he did throughout his life, Blessed Josemaría prayed to God for the people who were slandering him and the Work. In this way he put into practice our Lord Jesus Christ's teaching, "Do good to those who hate you, bless those who curse you, pray for those who abuse you."[6]

That Centre no longer exists. Another larger one took over from it, at 15 Villanueva Street (whose number was also later changed to 13 in a municipal reorganisation). It is still there and is one of the oldest in Madrid. Some of the people who had lived in Martínez Campos Street went to live there, and they were fortunate enough to have Blessed Josemaría visit them frequently and celebrate Holy Mass there.

Coincidentally, in the same building on Martínez Campos Street lived the family of the present Prelate of Opus Dei, Monsignor Javier Echevarría, who was still a child at the time.

---

[6] *Luke* 6:27-28.

14 Diego de León Street

But there were still plenty of activities being held in Jenner Street for which the residence was not really adequate, mainly because of the development of the Work in the year and a bit since the end of the Civil War. Another place was needed, for two purposes which the Father saw clearly as being urgent: one to set up a base for the government of Opus Dei; the other, to have a suitable place for the formation of the younger members of Opus Dei. In October 1940 some of the furniture was moved from the Jenner Street residence to a house at 14 Diego de León Street, which belonged to the heirs of the Marquis of Donadío.

The people who moved there were the Father, Grandmother, Aunt Carmen, Uncle Santiago, Alvaro del Portillo, Isidoro Zorzano, José Orlandis, and a very few more. I remember having seen the receipt for the rent of one of the first months: it was in Isidoro's name.

Among the furniture which was moved there from Jenner Street, that I remember, were the things from the guests' dining-room, which now became an ordinary dining-room. To these were added many other pieces of furniture, some of which had belonged to Grandmother and the families of some members of the Work, and some which had come from my parents' old house in Albacete. Among these last may be mentioned the furniture which has stood in the vestibule next to the Oratory ever since then; the bench and several matching chairs which were placed in Grandmother and Aunt Carmen's bedroom and living-room; the writing-desk in the Father's first office; a cupboard and some Tagalog swords, which my brother Pedro had bought from Don Jorge B. at an auction in Albacete,[7] and other things. But all of that was not enough for the whole house; little by little the necessary items were bought, mainly second-hand, as the need arose. One room was equipped as an office, with cupboards to store the few documents concerning the governance of Opus Dei, and a big table with seats around it. This room, which was also a committee-room for the Father and his Commission, was known as the secretariat.

Grandmother and Aunt Carmen once again took on the domestic work. The basic necessities for the Oratory, except an altar-piece, were completed in time for Midnight Mass on 31 December 1940. Isidoro and an electrician were still working on the lights until shortly before the Mass began. But as I said, the Oratory did not yet have its altar-piece, which had been ordered from the workshop of the Albareda brothers, from Aragon. On 23 February 1941, in the Mass celebrated by the Bishop of Vitoria, Monsignor Javier de Lauzurica, the Blessed Sacrament was finally reserved in the tabernacle.

The altar-piece finally arrived in 1942 and was set in its place. It was a landscape, with six pictures,

---

[7] See Pedro Casciaro, *Dream and your dreams will fall short*, pp. 226-235.

three representing the Archangels St Michael, St Gabriel and St Raphael, and the other three the Apostles St Peter, St Paul and St John. In the centre there was a large picture of our Lady, seated. The work of the Aragonese artists fulfilled its aims very well and inspired devotion. The Father and the others liked it. Additionally, Fernando Delapuente touched up our Lady's face and repainted St Gabriel's. The picture is still in the same place.

In the academic year 1940-41 the central heating did not work, because it needed to be repaired and there was no money for repairing or maintaining it. The winter of 1940-41 was especially cold. The rooms on the ground floor and the first floor, which were the main rooms of the house, had very high ceilings, which made heating them still more difficult. The people who lived there had to put up with intense cold.

Alvaro del Portillo's smile

Those of us who lived in Jenner Street often used to go to Diego de León Street. There we used to meet Alvaro del Portillo, among others, who had been Secretary General of the Work since shortly after the Civil War. I remember how he never failed to look at us whenever we crossed his path. Alvaro never lacked a smile, a frank smile, full of affection, which radiated joy and peace. It had already become a constant feature of his, and he never lost it.

Later on, in the early 1950s, I again had the opportunity to see him frequently, in Rome, in the

Roman College of the Holy Cross. Don Alvaro still smiled whenever he looked at us. It was unquestionably a sort of external, undisguised sign of his genuine affection. But that virtue was founded on resilience and fortitude. He reprimanded me several times in the course of those years, clearly and charitably. I could recount some of those reprimands and corrections here, but it would mean jumping several years and breaking the thread of the present narrative. Don Alvaro corrected people whenever it was necessary, without passing over something wrong and without ever losing his tone of supernatural affection: one was left feeling thoroughly chastened but at the same time happy and grateful.

Letters

Those of us who had more free time were occasionally given other small jobs to do in Diego de León. There was one I particularly liked. Alvaro or José Luis Múzquiz were the people who usually asked us to do it. It was the job of writing to the few Centres of the Work in different cities in Spain, with pieces of news: telling them things that had happened in Jenner, giving a summary of a meditation by our Founder, passing on news that reached us from the other cities about the development of the apostolic activities.

In short, they were the sort of letters which the members of any family might write to each other. We used to leave one side of a page blank for Alvaro or

José Luis, or the Father himself, to add something a bit more substantial. They were nothing new in the history of the Work: letter-writing had been going on since the beginnings, not just between the faithful of Opus Dei but between all those who in one way or another took part in the Christian formational activities which had taken place in the Ferraz Street residence, or during the Spanish Civil War.[8] These letters helped keep up people's solidarity and friendship, and helped them practise the Christian doctrine of the Communion of Saints very deeply. This was referred to in *The Way*: "Son, how well you lived the communion of saints when you wrote: 'Yesterday I *felt* that you were praying for me!'"[9] And, "Someone else who knows of this 'pool' of supernatural riches tells me: 'That last letter did me a world of good: I could feel everyone's prayers behind it... and I need their prayers very much.'"[10]

In return, in our family gatherings in Jenner or Diego de León we would read the news they sent us from Valladolid, Valencia, Barcelona, or Saragossa, or from other parts of Spain. This exchange of letters has been adapted to suit present-day numbers and the spread of the Work and has never ceased since those times.

While I was doing this letter-writing and other

---

[8] See, for example, Pedro Casciaro, *Dream and your dreams will fall short*, pp. 219-223.
[9] *The Way*, 546.
[10] *The Way*, 547.

secretarial work, I was impressed by how intensely José Luis Múzquiz worked: he never wasted a minute. He spoke no more than was necessary, not digressing onto any subjects not directly related to the actual work in hand. And yet he was never too rushed to do apostolate or to explain aspects of the spirit of the Work to us. He never showed any desire to rest, or do sport, or take a walk, unless it was in order to talk to some young man so as to help him think more deeply about his responsibility as a Christian and his possibilities of doing apostolate among his friends and colleagues.

Charity and affection

These family letters are one among many aspects of the human and supernatural warmth which the Father infused into Opus Dei, as a result of a special foundational charism. Blessed Josemaría was a man who knew how to love. This means that he loved with all the depth of a love that is at once supernatural and human.

In a meditation during those months I heard him say something that made a deep impression on me. He related the story of a young woman who was ill and was being looked after by some good nuns. When a priest went to see her to give her spiritual care, he asked how she was. She replied that she was all right, that she was being well looked after and did not lack anything, but she added, "Here they treat me charitably, but my mother treated me affectionately."

The Father took this little story as a starting-point to explain what our fraternity was like in the Work: full of supernatural love, charity, but imbued with human affection, real, self-sacrificing affection, without any pious pretence but coming straight from the heart; affection which puts its heart into big things and little details alike, which radiates a warmth that is at once fraternal, fatherly, and motherly. This sort of divine-human love is not merely what shapes the way the members of the Work treat each other in daily living, but it also gives colour and joy to their lives, with the confidence that other people are there to support them when needed, while always avoiding the slightest interference in the professional sphere, which is an exclusively personal responsibility.

Of course this way of understanding and practising fraternity gave me a profound sense of security when I was with the Father and my brothers, and has done so from the very first time right up until the moment I am writing these pages. It was practised like that at the beginning of the Work, in the warmth of the Father's physical presence; and it is still practised like that now, in the warmth of his spiritual and human legacy, a family inheritance. But this is not just my impression: it is something that has been experienced by people who have met Blessed Josemaría and his spiritual children. It is what my mother, for example, found when she met "Pedro's friends".

The joy of being with the Founder of Opus Dei

The joy of Blessed Josemaría and the other members of the Work also impressed me deeply from the time of my first contact with Opus Dei. What I saw was not something merely natural. Blessed Josemaría had written, "The cheerfulness you should have is not the kind we might call physiological good spirits – like the happiness of a healthy animal. You must seek something more: the supernatural happiness that comes from the abandonment of everything and the abandonment of yourself into the loving arms of our Father-God." [11] Then and later I very often heard him say a short phrase which sums up the deepest root of joy: "Being sad is for people who don't know they are God's children".

Blessed Josemaría, as can clearly be seen in the biographies that have been written of him, was a joyful man, right from the very first times when he felt that God was asking him for something – and he was absolutely generous, not refusing him anything that he asked. He overflowed with supernatural joy and spread it to others. To be near him, join in conversations with him, and listen to his preaching, was always stimulating. He was very demanding with reference to the fulfilment of the Christian virtues, but that demanding approach was imbued with humanity and cheerfulness. Everyone who knew him agrees that one really enjoyed being with him, while at the

---

[11] *The Way*, 659.

same time one understood in greater depth the urgency of the struggle for Christian holiness, not just in general or in theory, but when it came to applying it to the specific details of every day and every moment. Amidst the adversities that God allowed him to undergo in order to forge his soul and make it steadfast, Josemaría Escrivá was at one and the same time profound, serious, and funny, because he lived by faith and love for God at every moment. Among the many supernatural charisms which God granted him were his cheerfulness and his humorous way of speaking.

"Pepe, you're getting as round as a barrel"

There comes to my mind a little story from about ten years after the period I am relating. It was at the beginning of 1952, not many months after my ordination to the priesthood. I had recently arrived in Rome, and at the age of twenty-eight I had what is called a healthy appetite. The different types of *pasta asciutta*, from spaghetti to macaroni, which form the basis for Italian cooking, were noticeably fattening, so that my cassock, which had been made some months before, showed up my "middle-age spread".

One day when I was standing with the Father, he said to me merrily, "Pepe, you're getting as round as a barrel." He was making me see, in a friendly and cheerful way but still very clearly, that I needed to moderate my appetite, or in other words that I needed to practise temperance better at meals.

This sort of supernatural joy is not something that belonged to bygone times: it is still thriving more than seventy-five years after Opus Dei was born, and we have the sure hope that with God's grace it will continue to give its serene warmth to the hearts of all the men and women who follow Blessed Josemaría's teaching: "I want you to be happy always, for cheerfulness is an essential part of your way. Pray that the same supernatural joy may be granted to us all."[12]

When Blessed Josemaría was explaining the unlimited scope of supernatural joy, I heard him say several times, almost literally, "'And, Father, if they break my head, will I still have to be happy then?' 'Yes, my son, you will, because that'll be a sign that God wants you to go around with a split head.'"

Later on I sometimes thought over the joy that had made such an impression on me when I met the Founder and the first people in the Work. It seems to me that it perfectly matches what we know of the first followers of Jesus Christ, as described by St Luke in the *Acts of the Apostles*;[13] and the Christian writings from the beginning of the second century. Among

---

[12] *The Way*, 665.
[13] e.g. "And day by day, attending the temple together and breaking bread in their homes, they partook of food with *glad and generous hearts*" (Acts 2:46-47). "Then they [the Apostles] left the presence of the council, *rejoicing* that they were counted worthy to suffer dishonour for the name" (Acts 5:41). "And when they came up out of the water, the Spirit of the Lord caught up Philip; and the eunuch saw him no more, and went on his way *rejoicing*" (Acts 8:39).

these, as just one example, I remember the *Shepherd of Hermas*. Through the whole of the book there runs a note of joy which flows from the main character and all who make up the visions. What is more, the same sort of rejoicing is seen in Hermas himself, following his conversion and his sincere fight to persevere and make progress in exercising the virtues despite his weaknesses.[14]

Devotion to our Blessed Lady

Another of the things which I remember being deeply impressed by from the moment I arrived in the Jenner Street residence was Blessed Josemaría's devotion and love for our Lady. As in every Christian family, when I was very little my mother had taught me to pray to our Lady and turn to her in my needs. However, I had never really grasped the depth of devotion to Mary. I remember, very gratefully now, how, when I arrived in Calatayud at the beginning of May 1939 and was a boarder in the Marist Brothers'

---

[14] E.g. *The Shepherd of Hermas*, Vision 1, II, 3-4: "And she said to me: 'Why are you gloomy, Hermas? You who are patient and good-tempered, who are always laughing, why are you so downcast in appearance and not merry?' And I said to her: 'Because of a most excellent lady [*viz* the Church], who says that I sinned against her.' And she said: 'By no means let this thing happen to the servant of God.'" Cf. also *The Shepherd of Hermas*, the whole of the Tenth Mandate; one could highlight one or two lessons from this chapter, such as, "'You are foolish, O man,' he said, 'and do not understand that grief is more evil than all the spirits, and is most terrible to the servants of God, and corrupts man beyond all the spirits, and wears out the Holy Spirit'", etc. (Translation by Kirsopp Lake, Loeb Classical Library, Heinemann-Macmillan, 1913.)

school, their celebration of Mary's month did me a lot of good. After the afternoon classes, they had Benediction of the Blessed Sacrament in the school chapel and said the Rosary and the Hail, Holy Queen. As the days went by the devotion of the Brothers and my classmates reached deeper and deeper into my heart. Perhaps God's grace was at work preparing my soul to receive further graces. However, I was not very persevering in practising what my mother and the Marists had taught me.

But from summer 1940 onwards the Father's constant teaching on practising devotion to Mary, and his own example, brought about a change in my carefree attitude. The Founder of the Work told us repeatedly, "I don't want you to imitate me except in the love I have for our Lady." Among the norms of piety our Founder impelled us to practise was the Holy Rosary. Theology has always maintained that habits are acquired by the repetition of acts. And this is undoubtedly what took place silently within my soul. A reading of Blessed Josemaría's writings shows to what degree he himself lived continually in our Lady's presence, and desired everyone to take account of our Lady constantly in their lives. But here I am only aiming to put on record the impact his devotion to Mary, a devotion at once sturdy and tender, made on me from the moment I came into contact with him.

Chapter Eight

Treasured memories
(Winter 1940-41)

Beginning of the academic year 1940-41

The apostolic horizon in Madrid had widened considerably since the previous academic year. In Jenner Residence several places had been freed by the opening of the two new Centres in Martínez Campos Street and Diego de León Street. I remember some parts of the leaflet which was printed to advertise the hall of residence and fill the vacancies. It described the residence and gave the rates: "Fees for one month, all meals included = 320 pesetas, plus a provisional increase of 15%". "This Residence is not for the idle or lazy..." And it spoke about the family atmosphere, study, freedom, and "healthy, plentiful food". Those of us who were living there comprised three broad groups: the people who had been there longest; then the youngest, who were students; and the third group was made up of a large number of new residents, filling up all the available places.

Among the veterans I remember Justo Martí, the director; Emiliano Amann, Carlos Arencibia, Angel Galíndes, Francisco Ponz, Jesús Larralde, and Juan

Antonio Galarraga. There were also many new people, most of them from the Basque country: Rafael Amann, Emiliano's brother, Félix Iñiguez de Onzoño, Javier Domínguez Marroquín, José Luis Saracho, Ignacio de Orbegozo...; from other parts of the country came Vicente Mortes Alfonso, Bernardo García, Francisco Martínez, and Magín Ferrer (all four from the Valencia region of Spain), Luis Fedriani from Seville, Alberto Frutos, José Ramón Madurga, Alfonso Villuendas, and Ignacio Ducay (all four from Saragossa), Manuel Lantero from Asturias, and many others whose names escape me after all these years.

Despite the absence of the Father and the older members of the Work, we tried to make sure that the atmosphere remained the same, though we did not think it would be an easy task. When the Centre at 14 Diego de León Street had opened, the rooms in Jenner Street were rearranged. A room that had been a larder became a tool-cupboard. Throughout Spain food was becoming extremely scarce and the ration-cards, soon to be notorious, were becoming all-important and were strictly controlled. By means of these ration-cards the Government was trying to ensure a fairer distribution of scarce foodstuffs so that, as far as possible, poorer people would not be deprived of them. The consequences of the Civil War, still in the recent past, and the Second World War were keenly felt: it was almost impossible to import food. Among the things which had been left in the former larder we found a tin labelled "Malt Substitute". Malt, of course, was itself a coffee substitute. We did not know what this second substitute consisted of. What we did know was the effort involved in finding nourishment and keeping prices down in those times of widespread poverty.

Despite these difficulties, we did succeed in giving the residence the same characteristics as it had had the year before: an atmosphere of serious study, a welcoming family style, and spiritual help for all the residents. As had become traditional from the times of the Ferraz Street residence, Christian formative circles were given, and the Father preached some meditations and talked to each of us individually from time to time. A chaplain came to celebrate Mass every day. Blessed Josemaría said it there a few times.

Because of the general impoverishment of Spain, our sports were almost entirely reduced to football, which we played as and where we could. Jesús Larralde discovered a playing-field near what is now the Santiago Bernabeu Stadium. We went there several times for a game. We used to call it "the Larralde Ground". At that time that part of Madrid was half deserted. Our enjoyment made up for the lack of facilities. Other sports were rowing on the lake in Retiro Park and going for short hikes outside Madrid, on free days. As for weekends at the Sierra de Guadarrama, that year we made no plans for them.

The Father and my studies in Jenner

As the Ministry had refused my request to sit the

seventh-year secondary education exam at the September examination sessions, I needed to follow the seventh-year course during the academic year 1940-41. There were various options open to me. One was to go back to my Uncle Diego's house in Barcelona, where he would be delighted to put me up and pay for my studies: this would involve a certain degree of dependence on him, and my family was not altogether happy with that fact. Another was to study the seventh-year course on my own in Torrevieja, staying with my paternal grandparents. But this option meant I would not be getting the best out of my studies, and I would be rather isolated. A third possibility, which was the one favoured by my brother Pedro, was to apply for a scholarship at the Patriarch Juan de Ribera Foundation in Burjasot, Valencia. My good academic record, and perhaps some friends who could give me good references, made it probable that I would win the scholarship. When Blessed Josemaría heard that we had set about applying for this, he recommended us to reconsider the matter: the strict rules for boarders and the demands made by the institute on its students meant that it might not be the best thing for my personal freedom and the specific formation I was acquiring during those first months of my life in Opus Dei.

Pedro had been thinking principally about the financial difficulties which had come up after the Civil War, since my father, in exile in Oran, was unable to pay for my studies. I do not know what

Pedro and the Father said to each other about all of this, but from what happened afterwards I realised that the Father must in some way have suggested that I should stay in Jenner Street to finish my schooling and Pedro, as my elder brother, should take on the financial burden of his younger brother's upkeep and studies. This meant in practice a serious commitment on the part of the Father himself with regard to my situation, and a sign of Blessed Josemaría's capacity for gratitude.

What I came to realise later was his immense gratitude for the fact that my parents had donated their furniture to the Work when they heard through Pedro about the complete destruction of the residence at 16 Ferraz Street. There was a lot of furniture, and some of it was very good quality: besides what they had bought themselves for their house in Albacete, my mother had inherited her parents' furniture (as both her brothers were still single and did not have houses of their own), and my father had been given some from an apartment my grandparents formerly owned in Madrid. This had all helped to furnish the Jenner Street residence and the Centre in Diego de León Street, and my father's library was now in our Founder's office and other parts of the house in Diego de León Street.

The short time I had been going to spend in Madrid with Pedro for the summer of 1940 was thus to be prolonged for at least eight months. This made me very happy, because it meant being near the

Father, at the heart of the Work. I was, however, the only student still in secondary education, surrounded by university students; but as a matter of fact this did not give me any serious complexes.

Finishing secondary education at the Ramiro de Maeztu Institute

For the academic year of 1940-41 I enrolled at the Ramiro de Maeztu National Institute for what was at that time the seventh and final year of secondary education. Pedro, who had taught in the same institute during the 1939-40 session, saw to the necessary formalities. The standards were high both academically and humanly, but I think I managed to adapt without any difficulty.

There were some excellent teachers there. The person who comes to my memory first is Don Tomás Alvira,[1] Professor of Natural Sciences. He had outstanding gifts as a teacher and an exceptionally good relationship with his students, without prejudice to the demands of the difficult subject he was teaching that year, geology, which included many classes on crystallography, a really tough topic if it had not been for Don Tomás's teaching qualities. He

---

[1] Tomás Alvira Alvira was born in 1906. As well as his teaching post at the Ramiro de Maeztu Institute he was a research scientist in pedology. When he reached retiring age he dedicated himself enthusiastically and efficiently to teacher training as the principal of the school of teacher training at the private institution "*Fomento de Centros de Enseñanza*" (Promotion of Educational Centres). He died in Madrid in 1992, his hands full of good works done for the benefit of others.

was a disciple and then colleague of Professor J. M. Albareda, and, like him, did research in soils. Don Tomás had been receiving spiritual direction from Blessed Josemaría for years. He had been one of the small group of people who crossed the Pyrenees into Andorra with the Father at the end of 1937. He was thoroughly in sympathy with the spiritual message of Opus Dei and at the same time felt he had a clear vocation to marriage, and the Father saw this too.

Tomás got married in 1939. Years later, when, in the canonical journey made by the Work, the Church opened the possibility of married people joining Opus Dei to seek holiness by fulfilling their commitments to their family and their work, God called Don Tomás to the Work as one of the first married members. And he granted him the additional grace that his wife soon joined the Work too, and that six daughters and two sons likewise asked to be admitted to Opus Dei. God knows best, and does things better than we could have planned!

Other notable teachers I had at the Ramiro de Maeztu Institute were: Don Luis Ortiz Muñoz, a consummate Latinist and the Principal of the Institute, who treated his students very humanely; Don Lorenzo Vilas, a thoughtful, intelligent, friendly man, who taught a rather odd subject that was on the curriculum in those days, a mixture of chemistry and physics and the basics of applied sciences for industry, commerce, and economics. Later on he became a university professor, I think at the Faculty of Pharmacy at Madrid, and director general of secondary education, towards the end of the 1950s. History of Spanish Literature was taught by Allué Salvador, who was cordial, understanding, and brilliant, an expert both in the subject he taught and, later on, in the highest positions in the National Savings Bank.

Gymnastics and sport

I will not proceed to describe all the teachers I had that year, but I do not wish to omit mentioning the gymnastics teacher, the athlete Guevara, a former record-holder for the high jump, who was also proficient in several fields in athletics, especially throwing the discus and javelin, and weight-lifting. He was thirty-six at the time and his muscles and physical strength impressed us. Above all, he made us feel the powerful attraction of athletics. Admittedly, my liking for the "king of sports" dated from before that time, almost from my childhood. A significant moment had been the film *Olympics*, which I saw at a special showing for students when I was staying in Barcelona. It was about the 1936 Olympic Games in Berlin. It was one of the films I loved most when I was young, and it had the greatest effect on me. But my liking for athletics was really limited to theory until it became enjoyment in practice thanks to Guevara the athlete: long-jump and high-jump, hundred-metre sprints – a speciality which helped me to be extremely quick on the football-pitch too – javelin-throwing, and discus-throwing were the types of athletics I practised most, trained by Guevara, a great master of athletics.

Finally, although he did not teach me, it is impossible to speak of the Ramiro de Maeztu Institute in those years without remembering another Latin teacher, Don Antonio Magariños. He was the director of studies and fulfilled his role with exemplary dedication: when we students raced in for our morning classes, Don Antonio was already there in the hall. At break times and games, there he was, always accessible. He encouraged the basketball team, which in those days was made up of the tallest and most athletic students from the top of the school. This sport soon came to be a major way for past students to keep in touch with one another and with the spirit of the Ramiro de Maeztu Institute: for years, the best players continued to play for the institute team after they had left the institute, taking part in progressively higher-level contests. This was the origin of the "Students" team, one of the most renowned of the first-division Spanish basketball teams; and, later on, of the Antonio Magariños Sports Centre.

Trip for school-leavers

When the school year was safely over, but before the redoubtable state examination, we seventh-year students went on a one-week school trip to mark the end of our studies. Allué Salvador was the teacher in charge, and he took great care of us; we behaved as responsibly as adults. The main place we visited was Galicia, where I had never been before. I was most impressed by the architecture of Santiago de Compostela, and the green of the Galician fields and hills, which contrasted with the dryness of La Mancha and the coasts of Alicante and Murcia where I had grown up.

In Galicia I managed to make contact with Alberto and Ramón Taboada, whom I had met in Jenner the summer before. I had one afternoon free during our trip. I spent it with them, and we prayed for a while with the help of *The Way*, at a spot just outside Vigo, with a view over the sea and Monte Castro. Both they and I found it a terrific experience in a part of Spain where there was as yet no Centre of the Work. It may seem totally insignificant now, but to us in those times it meant sharing in one aspect of the adventure we had embarked upon a year before.

Setting up Diego de León

They moved into the little house at 14 Diego de León Street in October. The house had obviously suffered from neglect during the three years of the Civil War, and there was a lot to be done. Their first concern was for the Oratory, then Grandmother and Aunt Carmen's room, the ground floor where people came in, and some of the bedrooms. Christmas was soon upon them. The Father was very keen to get the main work in the Oratory finished, sparing no effort to ensure that Mass could be said as fittingly as possible. They redoubled their efforts as the time for Midnight Mass approached.

The few of us who had stayed in Jenner Residence for the holidays, plus, perhaps, some of the people from the Martinez Campos Centre, went to Diego de León Street for the meditation before Midnight Mass on Christmas Eve. Unless my memory deceives me the Father gave the meditation and celebrated Mass. The next day many of us from Jenner went back there to join in a family get-together and celebrate Christmas. Though the decorating and furnishing were only half-finished, the house on Diego de León Street was beginning to prove its usefulness.

Juan Jiménez and the younger members

The Father took very special care of the youngest and most recent members of the Work. That included several of us in Jenner and others who were living with their families in Madrid. We would gather in Diego de León Street at about half-past six in the evening, several times a week. With the ideal of combating the cold, which was made worse by the house's lack of central heating, and in order to help toughen us up, Juan Jiménez Vargas took us all into the garden at the agreed time: coats, jackets, and ties off! Intense circuit training, alternating with short races, was enough to loosen up our muscles, get our hearts beating strongly, and work up some heat, all within a few minutes. At the end of that year, Juan Jiménez, who was doing research in human physiology, published a book on gymnastics and physical exercise. Perhaps he had been trying out his theories on us, and had found them confirmed by the good health it brought us.

After the intense physical exercise, we had a quick wash and went to have tea. Aunt Carmen prepared what she could, and what her ingenuity and experience suggested. If there were any leftovers from lunch she used them, duly re-worked and with suitable additions. Tea was a rapid affair, and we usually had it standing up, in the big dining-room. Afterwards someone would give us a formative talk about some aspect of the spirit of the Work.

A little before eight o'clock we would hurry back to Jenner (which only took a few minutes in those days, since the streets of Madrid were almost empty of traffic) to arrive in time to look after the doctrinal, formative activities with the students, which all used to be held in the hour or so before dinner. We had organised a number of study circles, to which we took residents and friends who wished to develop their Christian faith and practice by that means. The circles were rounded off by short, lively conversations in which we discussed national and international events from a Christian angle, especially those concerning the Second World War and the adventures of student life in the different faculties of the university and schools.

With Grandmother and Aunt Carmen

During the school year 1940-41, gymnastics and sports lessons and some practical classes at the Ramiro de Maeztu Institute finished at about five in the afternoon, and we left straight away. From my classmates, most of them born and bred in Madrid, I soon learnt the art of getting on and off moving trams. They were the old kind, with an open platform. Moreover, it was considered very bad form among ourselves to get on or off at a stop, as though it were somehow bourgeois or effeminate (such were the opinions of the times). When I finished at the institute I would look and see whether any of those trams was coming down Serrano Street, and if so I got on it in the way I had learnt. When it crossed Diego de León Street I got off in the same way. If there was no tram in sight I ran down the street. Either way it took me very few minutes to reach 14 Diego de León Street.

I then had a good hour before Juan arrived for the circuit training and races in the garden. I used the time to go to Grandmother and Aunt Carmen's room to see whether anything needed mending. In this way I carried on with my summer job in Jenner. Sometimes I was able to effect the repair there and then, if it was an electric iron, for example, or a sewing-machine or lamp. On other occasions Carmen would take me to the kitchen, the laundry, or the larder, where the problem was, or wherever it was necessary to make some modification to install some appliance. I enjoyed the opportunities this gave me to talk and listen to her.

On one occasion I had a three-cornered tear in my trousers below the knee. I went straight to Carmen to show her what had happened. She said, "Find yourself another pair of trousers and bring me those to mend." And so I did. While we were with Juan and his circuit-training, she actually re-wove the rip, so that the mend could hardly be seen even from close up. It is easy to understand how stimulating I found those little episodes, especially since my mother was in Oran with my father in exile. Perhaps for that same reason, Grandmother and Aunt Carmen lavished attention on me.

Grandmother's death

Those encounters with Grandmother and Aunt Carmen continued from October until just days before Grandmother's death.

Her illness was a short one. Towards the middle of April she went down with influenza. A few days went by, and she did not improve. Her condition began to cause concern, but nobody thought it might turn into something serious. However, in the end she took a turn for the worse. The doctor diagnosed double pneumonia, which was very dangerous in those days, before the discovery of antibiotics. On 20 April the Father went to take leave of Grandmother, worried about the direction the illness was taking, though the doctor had dismissed the idea that she might die. José Orlandis remembers that when he came out of her room Blessed Josemaría said to some people who were nearby, "I think Grandmother is very ill. But there are fifty priests waiting, and my duty is to go and attend to them."[2]

And he went to Lérida, where he had agreed to give a spiritual retreat to the clergy of the diocese, including the bishop. He knew the various prognoses for the illness, though he had hopes that she would recover. In any case, sick at heart, he left his mother in order to go and attend to the priests, heroically accepting that God was asking him to set an example, to anticipate what in time would happen to many of his children, who for the sake of serving God and souls would not be able to be at their parents' bedside in their times of crisis. I heard the Father himself express this conviction and resolution later on in private, with deep emotion.

Two days later, on the 22nd, Grandmother died in her room. It took all of us by surprise. We could not believe that God was going to take her so suddenly, because before she caught the influenza she had been very well. But what had happened was that the pneumonia, instead of abating, got worse, and the crisis came in a very few days. Before he heard the news, in the middle of the spiritual retreat for the clergy in Lérida, Blessed Josemaría preached a meditation about the mother of the priest, into which he poured his own experience and other people's for the

---

[2] José Orlandis, *Años de juventud en el Opus Dei*, Madrid, Rialp, 4th edition, 1994, p.126.

benefit of his hearers. Alvaro del Portillo telephoned the Father to tell him that Grandmother had died.

In a letter written in 1956 Blessed Josemaría tells of those moments: "In 1941, I left my mother very sick in Madrid, in order to go to Lérida to give a retreat to diocesan priests. I did not know how serious it was, because the doctors did not think that my mother's death was imminent, or that she might not be cured. 'Offer your aches and pains for this work I am going to do,' I asked my mother as I said good-bye. She agreed, although she could not avoid saying in a whisper: 'This son!...' On arrival at the seminary of Lérida, where the priests were doing their retreat, I went to the Tabernacle: 'Lord, look after my mother, for I am looking after your priests.'

Halfway through the retreat, at midday, I gave them a talk: I spoke about the supernatural work, the incomparable role, proper to the mother by the side of her son, the priest. I finished, and wanted to stay for a little while recollected in the chapel. Almost immediately, the bishop who was Apostolic Administrator, and also on retreat there, came up, his face quite visibly altered, and said to me: 'Don Alvaro is on the telephone for you.' I heard Alvaro say: 'Father, the Grandmother has died.'

I returned to the chapel, without a tear. At once I understood that the Lord my God had done what was most fitting. And I cried, as a child cries, praying aloud – I was alone with him – that long aspiration I so often recommend to you: *Fiat, adimpleatur, laudetur... iustissima atque amabilissima voluntas Dei super omnia. Amen. Amen.*[3] Since then, I have always thought that the Lord asked me for this sacrifice as an external sign of my love for diocesan priests, and that my mother continues to intercede for that work in a special way."[4]

We kept a vigil of prayer beside Grandmother with all the love and gratitude we were capable of. The coffin was placed in the Oratory of the Centre in Diego de León Street. The Father came back straight away. Because of the difficulties of public transport he accepted the offer of a car from Juan Antonio Cremades, the civil governor of Lérida at that time, who had been a friend of his since they were students in the Faculty of Law at Saragossa. But the car had a breakdown and got to Madrid at about two o'clock in the morning of the 23rd. Later that morning we went to give him our condolences one by one, almost wordlessly. They were moments of deep sorrow.

I remember that the Father received us in the hall outside the Oratory. It was the first time I ever saw him cry, and also the first time he gave me a prolonged embrace, almost hanging from my shoulders. We said hardly anything. I only said, "Father!" And he said little more than "Pepe!" Grandmother had been so very much to him, and to each of us too!

At that point I understood more than before

---
[3] *May the most just and most lovable Will of God be done, be fulfilled, be praised... above all things. Amen. Amen.*
[4] Blessed Josemaría Escrivá, *Letter*, 8 August 1956.

about how far the love of the Father's heart reached, how much he loved his mother and how much he loved us, his children, all together and individually, so that his really devastated heart found deep consolation in us. I also understood our Founder's deeply-felt paternity better, and I think that from then on I loved him still more.

Grandmother's legacy

Grandmother had died prematurely, at the age of sixty-four. I remember her in all her vigour: her face smooth, without a single wrinkle, just as she had been when I first met her two years earlier; she looked younger than her age. She was ever serene, ever busy with domestic work – looking after us – friendly and affectionate. She was delightful to talk to, typically Aragonese in her witty turns of phrase, with a fine sense of humour that was always full of charity and interest for one and all. Her piety was unostentatious and refined. Her judgement on the goodness of an act was unerring. She had a manifest life of faith and resilience in the face of adversity or just the discomforts and ordinary difficulties of life, and a tried and tested capacity for sacrifice.

The family air in the Centres of Opus Dei owes a great deal to Grandmother and Aunt Carmen. They started many of the homely details and aspects that are now handed down among the customs of the Work: things that began in the atmosphere of the Founder's parents' home, and continued and developed in our daily living with Grandmother. Her house in Madrid was the first place where traditions such as tidiness, care for the objects and furniture of the home, cleanness, elegance and simplicity of behaviour, all began. This is Grandmother's legacy. We all loved her enormously.

For years I have asked Grandmother for help when I lose some prized or necessary item. I have always found them again, in what seemed like impossible circumstances. It would take too long to recount them all. The latest were my copy of the *Liturgia Horarum* (the Breviary), a present from Monsignor Alvaro del Portillo when he was Prelate of Opus Dei, and my passport, on the eve of a journey abroad. The first was obviously something I valued greatly.[5] The second would have meant cancelling or delaying a journey which had been arranged, and changing the dates and times of conference bookings. My readers are free to do whatever they like when they lose something they value, but I recommend appealing to Doña Dolores Albás, Blessed Josemaría's mother.

---

[5] The reader will forgive me if I tell the story of losing the Breviary. One Saturday afternoon I took my mother, aged eighty-seven, for a walk near Pamplona. When we went back I left the book on the car bonnet while I helped her into the car, and then we drove off. That evening I missed the book. I went back the next day and combed the spot, but could not find it. I asked in the nearby village, Setoain, but no one had seen it. I went on to the next village, Errea. Here they did give me news of it: someone from the village had found it, but was away until the following Saturday. When I went back, he explained that on a sharp bend in the road he had noticed some horses' hoof-prints leading into a thickly overgrown area. Surprised, he stopped the car and followed the

Aunt Carmen

I cannot leave the subject without describing what Carmen was like. She possessed an extraordinary degree of finesse and elegance, both humanly and spiritually. Without belonging to the Work, she dedicated herself to it with total generosity from the moment Blessed Josemaría asked for her help, especially at the end of the Spanish Civil War. This dedication meant sacrificing her own daily plans and long-term aims in life. She knew that in those years the women of the Work were not yet able to take charge of the domestic running of the Centres since there were still very few of them, and also because the houses, usually rented, did not offer suitable working conditions or the necessary degree of independence for them. Carmen, first with Grandmother and then on her own, supplied this work, which was indispensable for the family atmosphere God wanted Opus Dei to have. God unquestionably rewarded her hidden sacrifice by giving her an inner joy which radiated outwards.

She loved us all like a mother does, without flattering us, but with steadfast affection, always managing to be in the right place at the right time. She was an excellent conversationalist, at the same time as with outstanding expertise and a capacity for

---

marks. A few yards away from the road he found the book, open. He thought it might belong to the priest he had seen earlier with his mother, and picked it up. Immediately after he had recovered the book, it started raining hard.

managing and doing domestic work, she got all the work done and administered her charge with the keenness and economy of the mother of a large and poor family. She renounced forming a home of her own, though she received several very good offers of marriage, simply to respond to the need that she saw, in God's presence, of helping her brother Josemaría and serving God in the way she judged best. We can never be sufficiently grateful for the help Grandmother and Aunt Carmen gave the men, and perhaps still more the women, of Opus Dei. Those of us who, like myself, were lucky enough to see all this with our own eyes, cannot fail to be deeply grateful and filled with admiration. To be frank, I must confess that since Carmen died in 1957 I have always prayed for her and Grandmother by name, together with my parents, in the *Memento* at Mass every day, although I am quite sure that they do not need my prayers.

Blessed Josemaría's visits

During the school year 1940-41 we saw less of Blessed Josemaría than in the times when he lived in Jenner Residence with us. But he was always able to add an affectionate note to chance meetings, such as passing each other in a passage at 14 Diego de León Street. The Father was ever-mindful of us. I mean that he never let us go past without looking at us directly and saying some little thing to encourage us to keep in God's presence and offer up what we were doing, or, simply, to help make life pleasant for us. He had the gift of always being able to say something relevant, full of supernatural sense and human wit.

Although it happened about twelve years later than all this, I cannot resist relating an amusing story from my stay in the Roman College of the Holy Cross. It must have been in 1953. In the Prelature's central offices in Rome there is a long vestibule called the "Galleria della Campana". One day I came into it at one end just as the Father was coming in from the other. We walked towards each other, and as we met, he said, and I think these were his very words, "Pepe. You're not short. Nobody could call you tall. But don't worry, you're not short." Obviously, together with his words there was also the tone of his voice and his gestures. It made me laugh, because it was so funny and unexpected. Of all the things I might have imagined him saying to me, I would never have thought of that. It showed the Father's love for one of his sons and his desire to encourage us even in the most ordinary and trivial things.

Isidoro Zorzano's hidden sacrifice

Ever since my walks with Isidoro and the science classes he had given me the summer before, I had naturally felt a tremendous respect for Isidoro: how he had managed to fit my needs into the many things he had to do! I had also noticed other virtues in him, such as his detachment, his humility, and his faithfulness to the Father, which was constantly manifest. For me Isidoro was an accessible, practical example of how to progress in the spirit of Opus Dei. Perhaps this was the reason why I was particularly struck by something our Founder said about him to two or three of us in Diego de León Street, at the height of the very cold winter of 1940-41. With reference to something I cannot now remember, he told us discreetly that, as a mortification, Isidoro was wearing a raincoat with no lining instead of an overcoat, in spite of the freezing weather and the fact that he was very sensitive to the cold.

With mortifications like this, Isidoro was following the centuries-old practice of the Church, of imitating in some way our Lord Jesus Christ's life of sacrifice, which culminated in His Passion. And in a deeply Christian way he had grasped the need to do penance for his own sins and for the offences committed against God by all human beings. But naturally that was just one of Isidoro's many mortifications and sacrifices, as I discovered. I started to notice more. I had seen his unfailing tidiness the summer before: how, without missing a single day, Isidoro left his room spotlessly clean and aired, with his bed made, and everything in perfect order. From the Founder of the Work he had learnt very directly to do ordinary things perfectly on the human level and give them supernatural meaning, self-sacrificingly; that is, to sanctify himself by fulfilling his tasks and duties, whether large or small, joyfully. That was what Isidoro had assimilated so well from the Father's teaching and example.

The Work's first canonical approval

On 19 March 1941 Opus Dei was approved as a Pious Union by the Bishop of Madrid, Don Leopoldo Eijo y Garay. Since its foundation in 1928 the Father had received the blessing and approval of the bishop of the Madrid diocese, in which the Work was born. It is well known that the essential features of Opus Dei did not fit into the Code of Canon Law which was then in force. The Father was worried in case canonical approval might have the effect of deforming those features. But because of the development of the Work, the serious slanders which were being spread about Blessed Josemaría, and the apostolic projects being undertaken by the faithful of Opus Dei, the need for official approval was making itself felt with progressively greater urgency. For this reason he decided to accept the above-mentioned approval proposed by the bishop. However, to ensure that it would not be prejudicial to the ultimate canonical form of the Work, he asked Don Leopoldo not to finalise its canonical constitution when he granted the approval. The bishop, understanding the reasons Don Josemaría explained, agreed to this.

Blessed Josemaría summoned those of us who were in Madrid to tell us about the approval. We went to Diego de León Street and he explained what this canonical step meant. He invited us to thank God and the Church very much for it, and particularly the bishop of Madrid. The Father was visibly delighted about it.

I remember now how some of us younger ones said to one another on the way out that all of that must somehow be important, because the Father looked so happy about it, and for the reasons he had explained to us. But as far as we were concerned, what our Mother the Church had done for us seemed quite obvious and natural, since we had given ourselves to God in order to place Him at the centre of our daily work, at the heart of all the honest endeavours of mankind. Later on I began to understand how simple-minded our response had been, because we were very young and quite ignorant of canonical affairs – though basically, and making allowances for that same youth and ignorance, perhaps we were also partly right in a way. For the rest, that step in Opus Dei's canonical journey, like the others which were taken in due course, did not change our way of life, nor the characteristics of our dedication, nor the apostolic tasks we were carrying out.

Chapter Nine

In full swing
(Summer – Autumn 1941)

Being a guide

The summer of 1941 in Jenner was different from the previous summer: the residence was not so crowded, because the intensive courses at the university had finished, and the Work Weeks were not held there either. What was similar were the frequent visits from people who had joined the Work in other cities.

Having finished my seventh-year schooling and taken the state examination in July, I was in a position to look after some activities which were being held in Jenner Residence. One aspect of this was something I had already done the previous summer, though in summer 1941 it was more fully developed: looking after people who came to spend some days with the Father, and showing them round the historic places where our Founder had carried out his apostolate with students and other young men before the Spanish Civil War. I talked about these places earlier, in Chapter Five.

Atocha Station

Besides acting as their guide, I took charge of obtaining their train tickets for their journey home. In those "times before under-development" one had to resort to tactics known only to people who were already familiar with Madrid. One such tactic, for example, was to enter into negotiations with a certain individual who ran a small private business, a kiosk in the forecourt of Atocha Station, where he sold newspapers and magazines, books, tobacco, etc. This man had friends who did him the favour of procuring tickets for him in summer-time, when they were very difficult to obtain. You had to win over the small-businessman, getting on the right side of him by means of a tip or two in passing, to oil the wheels. Obviously, I do not wish to enter into details. Perhaps my friend in the Atocha forecourt came to the conclusion that I was running my own little business too. As may be imagined, this activity took up quite a lot of time; the worst of it was that I kept having to reckon up accounts, and arithmetic has never been my strong point.

Moments with Blessed Josemaría

The occasions when I was able to see the Father were mostly the result of doing office jobs in the secretariat at Diego de León Street, as I mentioned in Chapter Seven.[1]

---

[1] See the section entitled *"Letters"*.

Another task I undertook was cataloguing the library which had been installed in Diego de León Street, to which new books were being added. Naturally, the work took time, especially since those of us who were doing it were by no means experts and were frequently doubtful as to how to proceed, though our doubts were never of any great importance.

While engaged on those activities we often saw the Father, and these encounters filled us with joy, since he always had some word of affection and guidance for us. In the same way, acting as guide for people who came to stay for a few days also meant an opportunity to be with the Father. He used these short meetings with his sons to speak to us, however briefly, about basic points of the spirit of the Work, taking little happenings or something we had told him, as his starting-point. For instance, if someone let a door bang shut it was an opportunity for him to teach us to put love for God, and care on the human level, into the smallest actions, upon which the holiness God wants of us is built up. Someone might relate a chance encounter, and he would take the opportunity to show us how we should see all the people we meet in life in an apostolic perspective, because "we are interested in a hundred souls out of a hundred," as he sometimes said, and we have to try to bring them to Christ. The discomforts of train journeys in those days was also an opportunity for him to speak to us about the spirit of sacrifice, "made joyously and cheerfully" for love of God, in which we should face up to any difficulty. Ours is "a smiling asceticism", which never destroys our cheerfulness, but "turns the prose of every day into hendecasyllables, heroic verse."

The María de Molina Centre

The activity carried out by Blessed Josemaría in Madrid was always enormous and he made frequent journeys, above all to spend time with the new children God was granting him for the Work. During the academic year 1940-41, quite a number of young men joined us, and we no longer all fitted in the Centres in Madrid. The Centre on Martínez Campos Street was no longer sufficient. A group of men had recently joined us who had started jobs, for whom there was no room there, and for whom the Jenner Street students' residence was no longer appropriate. A place was needed for them. At the end of the summer two adjoining apartments were knocked into one, in a newly-completed building at 115 Núñez de Balboa Street, on the corner with María de Molina Street, to make a place for them. By the start of the 1941-42 academic year it was already functioning. José Orlandis tells stories of the beginnings of this Centre which give a good idea of what it was like living there.[2]

Some of the people who had recently graduated went to live there, such as Amadeo de Fuenmayor,

---

[2] Cf. José Orlandis, *Años de juventud en el Opus Dei*, pp. 128-136.

José Orlandis, Vicente Rodríguez Casado, and Angel López Amo, as well as others who had been working for some time already, like José María González Barredo, Francisco Botella and Rafael Calvo, unless my memory deceives me. Manuel González-Simancas Lacasa, whom those of us who lived in Madrid called Manolo Lacasa, used to go to the Centre. He soon asked to be admitted to the Work and graduated as an architect a few years later. The Centre at María de Molina Street, then, was another ignition-point, a focal point of apostolic zeal, in an atmosphere of intense work. The preparation and moving in were done during the summer.

The first Centre of Studies

Blessed Josemaría's care for his sons, under the guidance of the Holy Spirit, knew no bounds. He was concerned for the development, on the spiritual, apostolic, human, and doctrinal levels, of all the young students who had been joining the Work. In Summer 1941 arrangements were finalised for the first Centre of Studies to start in October. Its aim (like that of all such Centres which would subsequently be set up in the most varied countries of the world) was to offer a period of intensive spiritual, human and doctrinal training to young members of Opus Dei, to give them a deep, practical knowledge of their specific vocational path in the middle of the world, and to enable them to carry out their apostolic mission properly. The Father saw clearly that our philosophical and theological training needed to be at least at the same level as our civil studies so that we could live out our Christian faith, as he phrased it, "with the piety of children and the doctrine of theologians", in accordance with God's plans.

To do this, he wanted to have them as close to himself as possible, especially at the beginning. In later years I have often linked this aim of the Father with the words St Mark's gospel gives: "And he [Jesus] appointed twelve, to be with him, and to be sent out to preach."[3]

The little house on Diego de León Street seemed to offer suitable conditions for this venture to begin. Besides the first and second floors, which were rather stately and suitable for receiving visitors, with the Oratory, a committee-room/office, one large dining-room plus a second one for visitors, there was also a big basement which could accommodate the kitchen, laundry, and store-room, and so on, for the domestic work, with a separate entrance at 116 Lagasca Street. On a third floor, well lit, there were a number of bedrooms, most of them with several beds, a large sitting-room, and a library/lecture-hall. The building had a small garden, where we had done gymnastics under the guidance of Juan Jiménez Vargas. To sum up, it was now possible to begin the in-depth training and development of a reasonable number of new members of the Work.

So in October 1941 the pupils of the first Centre

---

[3] Mark 3:14.

of Studies moved into 14 Diego de León Street, to live very near the Father and with the invaluable presence of Aunt Carmen, who managed all the domestic work of the house. Some of the first women of the Work came in at certain times to help Aunt Carmen in her work, and, since they were young, they learnt from her experience all they would need to know to do the housekeeping in both the men's and the women's Centres of Opus Dei in the future.

I lived there as a pupil of the first Centre of Studies, but only for the first term. After Christmas I moved back to Jenner Street. The Father appointed my brother director of the Centre of Studies. I was to live under the same roof as Pedro for the last time during the second and third terms of the academic year 1943-44 in Moncloa University Hall in Madrid, where again, he was the director and I was one of the residents, halfway through my course at the Faculty of Arts. After that I never lived in the same house as him except for the odd day or two in different places.

A fax from Mexico on Pedro's death

Because of all that I owe him on the human and supernatural planes, I feel moved to copy here some paragraphs from the fax which the Regional Vicar of the Prelature in Mexico sent me, in Spain, a few hours after Pedro's death in Mexico City.

"Mexico D.F., 24 March 1995

Dearest Pepe,

(...) Last night at 10.40 p.m. he left us to go to

heaven. Shortly before that many of us had gone to the Mass for Don Alvaro in the Basilica of Guadalupe, at which Cardinal Corripio presided. When I told him, before Mass, that Don Pedro was gravely ill, he asked us to make a special mention of him in the Prayer of the Faithful.

When Mass was over I went straight to his house. I got there just an hour before our Lord took him. People had been keeping him company there with special affection, all through that day, praying beside him to give him strength. Although he was barely conscious, he could hear what people were saying. For instance, he tried to make the sign of the Cross when he was given absolution.

After 5 o'clock he went into a coma. The whole time he was holding a rosary and the crucifix our Founder had given him when he asked for admission to the Work, which he kept all his life as a treasure. He was thoroughly well prepared, and, moreover, he had been purified by the truly heroic and supernatural way he endured his illness to the end (...).

After he died I celebrated the first Mass and telephoned the Father: he told me that we now have another saint in heaven, and that we were to pray for him a lot and also commit ourselves to his intercession. A few hours later we received a faxed letter from him.

To give you the gist of it, the Father told us that the coincidence of dates [Pedro died on 23 March, exactly a year after Alvaro del Portillo] showed that our Lord had been looking after him all that time and that Don Alvaro had received him into heaven personally. The Father said that for Don Pedro, a most faithful son to our Father, eternal repose would be a very high place in heaven, next to our Father and Don Alvaro, since he had always been very closely united to the person at the head of the Work; he also told us that recently Don Pedro had talked about how he desired to see the Blessed Trinity face to face, and our Lady had now granted him his wish. Finally, the Father encouraged us to carry on from the point where he left off, which is total fidelity, so as to do the Work as he did it, laying down his own life in the process.

The funeral was in the parish church of the True Cross. For nearly seven hours very many people prayed beside his body. There was a steady stream of people going up to kiss him and to pass rosaries and other objects through his hands. The atmosphere was one of immense affection and gratitude, with the emotion that everyone felt when they remembered how Don Pedro had spent himself to the very end, and that part of the many fruits of his generous, total dedication to his vocation were right there. I said in the homily that from Heaven he really could say "Dream, and your dreams will fall short", because now he was actually seeing it in God. When the coffin was carried out, everyone said farewell to him with a burst of thunderous applause (...).

With his death an epoch has come to an end in the history of the Work in this Region [of Mexico] – a singular, unique epoch. The Father has told us that from heaven he will help all of us a lot in our interior life and our apostolate so that we can reach many more people (...).

Rafael Fiol."

But to return to the memories of 14 Diego de León Street. The Centre of Studies began with few pupils. Among them I recall Jesús Arellano,[4] José Ramón Madurga,[5] José Javier López Jacoíste,[6] Vicente Garín,[7] and Ignacio Echeverría.[8] I do not want to give more names, because I am mixing them up in my memory with the people who started the following year, whom I joined for the whole of the academic year 1942-43.

---

[4] Jesús Arellano Catalán was born in Corella (Navarre). In 1946 he became Professor of Fundamentals of Philosophy at the University of Seville, where his work on both the professional and the human level went very deep, and where he remains as Professor Emeritus. He has many followers in this branch of learning.

[5] Born in 1922, he studied industrial engineering and furthered his studies in his speciality in Dublin, where he began the apostolate of Opus Dei. After being ordained to the priesthood he went to Japan to start the activities of the Work in that country, and is still there today.

[6] José Javier López Jacoíste was born in 1921. He was a notary and held professorships in civil law at several universities. He wrote works on civil law. He lived in Galicia, Spain, for many years. For some time now he has lived in Madrid.

[7] Vicente Garín, from Valencia, born in 1923, studied chemistry and was a renowned teacher in secondary education, to which he dedicated the whole of his life. He taught in the Gaztelueta School in Bilbao and is now retired.

[8] He comes from San Sebastián and studied chemistry; he went to Argentina in 1949, after being ordained a priest. He continues to exercise his ministry there.

The Father's care for the Centre of Studies

The first term of the 1941-42 academic year was a very special one for me. The Father gave us numerous meditations and we had a lot of informal family gatherings with him too, in which he explained many points of the spirit of Opus Dei. The foundation of everything was the sense of our divine filiation, which meant capturing and living the joyful reality of being God's children. On this basis it would be easier for us to achieve a life of prayer in the middle of the ordinary occupations of any Christian, to progress in our union with Christ our Lord and with each of the Divine Persons. We had to become "contemplatives in the middle of the world", so as to stay constantly in God's presence throughout the day, carrying out any activity, study, rest, manual work, or friendly contacts with our colleagues in a supernatural spirit and with apostolic zeal. In that way, the whole day would turn little by little into prayer: our different activities would be no obstacle to our active consciousness of God's presence, but on the contrary, they would be our way of meeting God. Then every day would become integrated into a "unity of life", combining our contemplation, our work and our rest, our apostolic tasks, joys, difficulties, and so on, into an indivisible whole.

And together with the life of prayer, making this 'unity of life' possible, we needed to have a spirit of penance, mortification, and sacrifice in the big or little events of every day, "offering the setbacks of the day to God". By following that line we entered more deeply into the sanctifying value of ordinary work, which is the hinge on which the spirit of the Work, and its theological and apostolic message, turns.

Aspects of life in the Centre of Studies

We always prepared for the daily celebration of Holy Mass with great care for the liturgy, and we sang, which helped us to penetrate the depths of the Holy Sacrifice. A devout priest, Don Enrique Masó, a great friend of Blessed Josemaría's and an expert in sacred music, was our singing teacher. He was very happy to see the interest we took in his classes, although at the outset he had to work hard to give us some kind of sensitivity and taste for music, which many of us completely lacked. To begin with our voices actually hurt his ears, but we soon acquired a better-modulated tone. It may have been he who composed or re-arranged the music for Psalm II, which we sang after Mass every Tuesday. Don Enrique officiated at the Exposition and Benediction of the Blessed Sacrament on liturgical solemnities, and began the singing of the *Salve Regina* on Saturdays.

The classes of Christian doctrine were taught by different teachers, all intellectually brilliant, and other priests who were friends of the Father. I remember especially the classes given by Don José María Bueno Monreal, who became Cardinal Archbishop of Seville years later, who taught us Fundamental Theology and Apologetics. He explained the proofs of the existence of God from Aristotle and St Thomas unhurriedly and, without heat, exposed the errors of the "adversaries" of the philosophical and theological foundations of the Christian faith. When I was serving as second-lieutenant in the infantry in 1946-47, I spend several months in Jaca, Huesca, where Don José María Bueno Monreal was bishop. I went to visit him a number of times. He received me warmly and spoke to me of the deep affection and admiration he felt for our Father, whom he looked on, not just as a friend, but as his elder brother.

I found the logic classes very hard. Metaphysics was more interesting and included contributions from Jesús Arellano, who was completing his course in pure philosophy at the university at that time.

We studied this philosophy and theology at the same time as our own subjects at our respective schools and faculties, and combined all this with our apostolate with our fellow-students and friends. It was an intense life, in which we had to make the fullest use not just of every hour but of every minute. But the Father encouraged us, often coming up to the third floor where we spent most of our time when at home.

Until the first three priests of Opus Dei were ordained in 1944 from among the numerary members, Blessed Josemaría was the only priest. Out of refinement, he did not want to hear our confessions, so that the sacramental seal should not encumber any aspect of the governance and the spiritual guidance he imparted to us. This was an attitude he always maintained. We used to go to confession to whichever priests we chose or were available. A current phrase in those days was "to go to confession to Father Happen", meaning the first priest one happened to find. I remember that during my previous stay in Jenner Street I used to go the nearby church of San Fermín de los Navarros, where the good Franciscan fathers ministered to penitents very well.

When the Centre of Studies began the Father took steps to ensure that we would not have to spend time going to and from churches if we did not want to. He invited Fr José López Ortiz, O.S.A., and Fr Aguilar, O.P., to come and administer the sacrament. Fr López Ortiz was a close friend of his, Professor of History of Law at the university, and years later became Bishop of Tuy-Vigo; Fr Aguilar had studied architecture before entering the Dominican order and was also a friend of his. Both of them knew the spirit and nature of the Work very well and were therefore in a position to help us on our way.

Over the years Blessed Josemaría told us countless times that we could go to whichever confessor we chose in any church; we had unlimited freedom of choice, like every member of the Catholic Church. We have always followed this in teaching and in practice, even now, when we have all the facilities within the Prelature because of the relative abundance of priests and, above all, because they are constantly willing to attend to us. In practice, the faithful of

Opus Dei do go to priests of the Prelature for confession, because they are living the same spirit as we are; and if possible we go to the same one every time, so that he can help us because he knows our personal circumstances better.

On frequent confession

One day when I was going out of Diego de León, I went to the Oratory to say good-bye to our Lord in the Blessed Sacrament as usual, and in the hall outside the Oratory I met the Father with two or three other people. I went forward to greet him, and realised I would not be getting in the way if I joined them. Blessed Josemaría was talking about the Sacrament of Penance. At one point he said that experience had shown that when people delay going to Confession out of carelessness, from that very moment they would almost certainly start to give up in their ascetic struggle and grow slack in practising the virtues and fulfilling their Christian duties. In order to have a close, personal relationship with our Lord we needed to have the sensitivity to wash our souls often: as a practical guide, once a week, or as often as we felt it was necessary. This was not just a suggestion made in passing: throughout the whole of his life Blessed Josemaría taught about the spiritual benefits of frequent confession, through which we can "play the role of the prodigal son", certain of always receiving God our Father's forgiveness.

Starting university

Like most students, I began my classes at university with great enthusiasm – perhaps more than most, because I had spent the preceding year as the only secondary-school student in a hall of residence full of university students. After thinking about it and consulting I know not how many people, I chose to take an Arts degree.

What I really liked most of all was aviation. During the years of the Spanish Civil War I grew enormously fond of it. I even acquired a dossier with the technical specifications of the fighter aircraft used by both sides. The dossier had been produced in a limited edition by the Republican Government Air Command, for the benefit of its pilots and the officers of anti-aircraft batteries. Near Albacete was a military airfield called "Los Llanos", which became a training school for pilots in the red zone. The trainee pilots used to stroll into town during their free time, and I was sometimes able to talk to them. I managed to learn the features of the fighter aircraft and even made wooden models of some of them. My ambition was to become an aeronautical engineer and one day, perhaps, design aircraft prototypes.

But when the time came to choose a university course I think that God made me understand the reality of my situation, which, since my father was in exile, was economically precarious. Getting into engineering school was a long, expensive process. It was a luxury I could not afford. I realised that doing a course in aviation was a mere pipe-dream, and decided to take an Arts degree, also having a great fondness for arts subjects. I never even talked to anyone else about the idea of doing aeronautical engineering: I thought it unnecessary to do so, and it was buried among my adolescent dreams. So I opted for an Arts course, in which the first degree only took four years in those days and involved minimum outlay.

The buildings of the Madrid University Campus were still under repair, having been severely damaged because the battle-front had been held up there for a long time. So, for lack of space, the classes of the Faculty of Arts were held in the lecture-halls of the old building on St Bernard's Street, from three till six in the afternoon. After Christmas, living in Jenner Street again, I was nearer the university: by running diagonally through the streets I was there in a few minutes. This was long before the days of jogging, but some of us practised it even then as an economical means of transport.

Years later my brother Pedro expounded his theory on sport to me. He divided it into intransitive and transitive. The former is practised when there is no pressing need for it: for example, today's sport of jogging, which he described as running to a place where there is no need to go. Transitive sports include running to class, because one has to get there anyway and by practising it one gets there sooner and more cheaply.

The scheme of studies in the Arts Faculty at that time consisted of two distinct cycles: two years of common subjects and then two of special ones. In the first cycle all the subjects were compulsory except for a choice between Greek and Arabic, and one between English and German. I chose Arabic (perhaps because it sounded more exotic) and German (because I had already done English at secondary school, but knew no German at all). The German classes were almost traumatic for me at the beginning, because the others had all done it at secondary school. The choice of Arabic had a lasting effect on me because years later, after my ordination, I dedicated myself to Scripture studies, which have been the focus of my intellectual work for the past forty years. Knowledge of the structure of Arabic is the key to understanding the other Semitic languages, such as Hebrew and Aramaic, which are a basic essential for biblical studies.

Teachers in the Arts Faculty

Despite the gaps which the Civil War had left in the ranks of teachers, which remained unfilled, the Arts Faculty at Madrid was striving to regain the high level of university teaching it had reached in the years before the conflict. Certain prominent figures, such as José Ortega y Gasset and Claudio Sánchez Albornoz, were no longer there. But some others continued to teach, like Miguel Asín Palacios, Manuel García Morente, and to some extent Xavier Zubiri. Others who were somewhat younger were beginning to shine with their own light so that at the beginning of the 1941-42 academic year I found some excellent teachers in the Arts Faculty.

The person who made the most impact on the direction of my studies in those years of my youth was unquestionably Don Emilio García Gómez,[9] Professor of Arabic, a disciple of Asín Palacios and a brilliant continuator of the school of Spanish Arabic specialists. Later on he was Principal of the Royal Academy of History for many years. I found his classes fascinating because of their depth, which revealed unsuspected horizons of scientific research, while the tone he gave them was pleasant and attractive. Another great teacher was Don Diego Angulo, Professor of History of Art. With his high level of academic attainment and serious commitment, communicated in his marked Seville accent, he awakened in us an interest for his subject. He taught two classes a week on the history of architecture and sculpture, in the old building on St Bernard's Street, and a third on the history of painting, in the first afternoon class on Fridays, which he held in the Prado Museum, often in front of the very paintings themselves.

The classes of another professor, Don Antonio

---

[9] Don Emilio García Gómez was born in 1905 and died in 1995, just a few days before his ninetieth birthday, having enjoyed a flourishing old age. He was one of the most brilliant and renowned figures of twentieth-century Spanish intellectual life. His research on the poetry and history of Muslim Spain was widely acclaimed.

Ballesteros Beretta, were a model of competent exposition. He was in the final years of his academic life and had attained the mastery that came of a whole life dedicated to teaching and research. He brought historical figures to life with the expressive gestures which accompanied his explanations. Don Juan Tamayo, professor at the Institute of St Isidore and auxiliary teacher in the Faculty, treated us with exquisite courtesy and explained the themes on the programme in an orderly, pleasant way, making it easier for us to learn the immense subject of the History of Spanish Literature, in which our textbook was the exhaustive manual by Juan Hurtado and Angel González Palencia, which we nicknamed "Little John" because of its thickness and after the first of its two authors. But I do not want to spend longer on my teachers at the outset of my university studies. I owe a great deal to all of them, and to my fellow-students as well.

The Father and my option for biblical studies

The following year, at the end of the common subjects in the Arts Faculty, I had to choose my specialisation. I was not sure whether to choose History or Semitic Language. I was in a considerable state of indecision, especially over the possibilities of jobs at the end of each. I consulted several different people. One day in Diego de León Street, when I was asking Don José Luis Múzquiz what he thought of it, the Father came in and was interested by our conversation. He listened for some moments before intervening. Although he left it entirely up to me to choose one specialisation or the other, he showed that he thought Semitic Language would be a good idea. "Like that," he said, "it will be a useful preparation for becoming a teacher of Sacred Scripture one day." I had never thought of this possibility, and, besides, I knew very little about it. He said nothing further on the question of becoming a teacher of Sacred Scripture.

Years later, when Blessed Josemaría asked me whether, in all freedom, I was willing to be a priest, and I said yes, he then said that I had made him very happy and that after being ordained I would go to Rome to take a degree in Sacred Scripture. I had almost forgotten the reason which had decided me for Semitic Language years earlier, but the Father had not. And a few months after my ordination, during a journey he made to Spain at the end of the summer in 1951, he told me, "Get your passport and everything else ready so that you can come to Rome, to study Sacred Scripture this year." So I did. I have never ceased to admire Blessed Josemaría's foresight and his persistence in following through a well-considered plan, never forcing matters, but making use of his sons' tastes and circumstances.

An irrelevance

As I write these pages on the beginning of my time in the Centre of Studies in Diego de León Street, an irrelevant episode comes to mind. It must have been in November 1941, when the director of the Centre of Studies, who at that stage was my brother Pedro, gave Jesús Arellano and myself a job to do. It was a fairly simple though somewhat laborious one. Jesús, as the older and more responsible of the two, was the one who was actually told what to do. According to him, we had to hire a hand-cart, go to the Centre in Vallehermoso Street, collect a large table, take it to the women's Centre which was just being set up in a house at 1 Jorge Manrique Street, leave it there, collect another one and bring it to Diego de León Street. In principle it all seemed very simple. But we encountered our first difficulty. The table would not fit through the front door or any other entrance of the house on Jorge Manrique Street. We had to take it apart and then put it together again when we had got it inside. Once we had completed this operation they showed us the other table. To me it looked exactly the same as the one we had just brought, but my colleague thought there was a slight difference. We took the second table apart, brought it out of the house, put it together again, and transported it to Diego de León Street. These operations took us the whole afternoon. When we finally arrived we informed the director that we had brought the table.

"The table?" he exclaimed. "You mean the tables."

We insisted that there was only one, and explained our manifold activities. Then he explained that the two tables were identical and as such had been intended for the library/lecture-hall of the Centre of Studies. And, rather disappointed, he added, "It's my fault for having given the job to two arts students."

We had to go back the next day, hire the hand-cart again, take apart and put together the original table, and bring it back. The odd time when I reminded Jesús Arellano of our exploit, he declared he did not remember any such thing. But it was a mistake that I found hard to forget.

Christmas holidays 1941-42

Quite a number of the people from the Centre of Studies in Diego de León Street went to spend a few days in their home towns. There were empty places, and Blessed Josemaría made use of this fact to hold a retreat for some university students who had been coming regularly to the Christian formative activities in Jenner Street. There were not many of them, about seven or eight. Those of us who were left in the Centre of Studies went to Mass and had our meals together with them, in silence, obviously. For the rest of the day we also tried not to make a noise or distract them. In this way the house which had formerly belonged to the Marquis of Donadío was put to full use, and since we had not yet got a conference centre, it took the place of one.

Blessed Josemaría received a lot of people of all ages. Some came from time to time to ask for his advice. Others came to him regularly for spiritual direction. We also used to see several ecclesiastical friends of his, either as guests for a meal or simply coming in to visit him. But all of this did not stop him from frequently coming up to the third floor, where the people in the Centre of Studies were, to spend time with us that Christmas too.

Ten-page letter

I think it was about then that our Father met me one day in the Centre at Diego de León Street and asked after my parents, who were in exile in Oran. The conversation soon led him to ask another question, which was, more or less, "How long is it since you last wrote to them?"

I had to reply, "Perhaps a month and a half now, Father."

Blessed Josemaría gave me a thorough telling-off, pointing out to me that my parents' greatest joy, in the situation they were in, was to get letters from me telling them about how my studies were going, and other details about my life. Therefore it was a serious fault against justice and charity towards them. And he wound up with something like, "Go and write them a letter ten pages long, on both sides, straight away. When you've finished it come and tell me."

I did not realise at that point that ten was a figure named at random, within the rebuke which was perfectly serious. I started writing and covered one, two, three... up to seven sheets of paper on both sides. And then I could not think of anything further to write. After trying for a time without knowing what I could add, I took the letter to the Father and told him how many pages I had written, and that I could not think of anything else to tell them. He did not look at the letter; he answered that that was enough, and told me to go and post it straight away. And he warned me that the whole episode should serve me as a guide in the future, not to delay keeping my parents up to date with my news.

I had in fact committed a fault against the fourth commandment, which Blessed Josemaría had termed "the sweetest precept" in his very earliest writings. And I understood that however much work I had, the task of writing to my parents was among the most sacred of all; I ought not to consider it a mere obligation but a joyous duty. My behaviour had sprung from a wrongly-understood "detachment", completely contrary to the spirit of the Work. The basic reason for it was nothing other than disorganisation and laziness.

Ignacio de Orbegozo

After Christmas I moved back to Jenner Street. Among the new residents was Ignacio de Orbegozo,[10]

---

[10] Ignacio de Orbegozo y Goicoechea was born in 1923. He worked as a surgeon for several years. He was ordained a priest in 1951. He got his doctorate in theology at the Lateran University in Rome in 1956. In 1957 the Holy See entrusted the Prelature of Yauyos, Peru, to his care. He was ordained a bishop in 1964. In 1968 he became Bishop of Chiclayo, Peru, where he exercised his pastoral ministry until his death on 5 May 1998.

a medical student. He was an open, friendly person from Bilbao, good at sports and very amusing. I heard that when he first came to the residence someone told him that if he wished he could come to the Holy Mass, which was celebrated every morning in the Oratory. But perhaps he wasn't told the correct time, which, unless my memory fails me, was seven-thirty. Before that, at seven o'clock, a fairly large group of us would begin a period of meditation together, with the help of readings from some spiritual book, such as *The Way*. Ignacio turned up in the Oratory punctually at seven o'clock for several days running, to find that every so often someone would read a few paragraphs aloud. After a few days, at breakfast one morning he said something like, "If the priest comes half an hour late to say Mass every day, wouldn't it be better to fix the time of Mass at half-past seven, once and for all?" (Obviously, he thought that the reading aloud was just in order to keep people occupied until the priest got there.) Someone explained the misunderstanding to him, and from the following day onwards he arrived at seven o'clock as before, but this time knowing what people were there for. He soon swelled the numbers of those of us who belonged to the Work.

Chapter Ten

University life to the full
(January – August 1942)

Jenner again

In this chapter I shall talk about what happened in Jenner Residence during the two remaining terms of the academic year. I had fewer opportunities of meeting Blessed Josemaría than before, since we were now living in different places. Being fully taken up with the activities in the residence and the atmosphere of the Faculty of Arts, I was not summoned to go and do little jobs with the Father or in the secretariat, nor to mend things for Aunt Carmen. However, I did find several good reasons for going to Diego de León Street.

Jenner Residence was in full swing, but now that other Centres of the Work had opened in Madrid, the number of faithful of Opus Dei who lived there had noticeably diminished. In a way I was now one of the veterans. On the other hand, the number of residents who were not in the Work had obviously gone up. Looking after these newcomers so that they felt at home, and did not miss their families or their home town on leaving them for the first time, took up quite a lot of time on the part of us older ones.

There was, of course, a good base of a few of the older residents from the times of the residence at 48-50 Ferraz Street; others had stayed on since the first times in Jenner Street. They were a great support in creating a good atmosphere in the residence. But most of the people were new. The majority were studying for the entrance examinations to the Schools of Engineering or the Schools of Architecture. They were good, hard-working students and were generally absorbed in their work, concentrating entirely on preparing for the entrance examinations, which in those days were extremely tough, and completely immersed in the huge quantity of study they had to do, especially a long list of mathematics or physics problems that their respective colleges set them for homework every day.

All this was basically a good thing. The message of Opus Dei about Christian sanctification through ordinary work found a good basis in that atmosphere of intensive study. The question was how to teach them to supernaturalize the efforts they were putting into it, and not to let themselves get carried away by worrying about the entrance examination results and, in some cases, by ambition and the desire for a personal triumph. Many of them stayed up to study after the evening meal, which meant they did not get enough sleep. We had to work hard to get them to rest and do any sports on Sundays, because they were so obsessed with studying and so inexperienced that they often failed to get any fresh air even on their free days.

In the course of those months the Father came a few times, though not as often as we wanted him to. As he had done the year before, he spoke to a lot of the boys and preached some meditations and days of recollection. Each visit from the Father warmed the atmosphere and was a stimulus for us in organising the activities which were held in the residence. The academic year 1941-42 was a new experience in our apostolate and our own lives; a very interesting experience, but perhaps a hard one for some of us.

Study circles and visits to "Our Lady's poor"

As we had done from the start, we gave Christian formative classes and circles in small groups in the residence. The people who came to these were those residents who freely wanted to and other students from outside, our fellow-students in the various faculties, schools, and colleges. When a particular group increased as new friends joined in, we would divide it into two. Almost all the members of Opus Dei used to give at least one circle a week. We were also helped in this task by some people who came from other Centres of the Work. I remember the first day Jesús Arellano, who was living in Diego de León Street, came to a circle bringing a fellow-student, Antonio Millán Puelles, who was to be a well-known philosopher in the future. I remember this particularly because by that stage they were both specializing in philosophy, while I was merely in the first year of the foundation course in the same faculty.

Their presence was an honour for the little group in that circle, who were mostly right at the beginning of their university studies.

The circles were complemented by visits to "Our Lady's poor", which was a long-standing tradition among the students who came to the apostolic activities run by faithful of the Work under Blessed Josemaría's guidance. At the end of every circle a collection-bag was passed round in which each of those present put however much money he thought suitable, according to the light God gave him. The bag we usually used in Jenner was made of a dark red velvety material. The money collected was distributed among the people who were going to make visits to poor people living on the outskirts of Madrid, whom they prayed for to our Lady, committing them to her motherly care. They used it to buy cakes and other such things that presumably the people they were visiting never otherwise had; so, children and adults alike could enjoy these delights, which were prohibitively expensive for them in their extreme poverty. We would agree on a day in the week, generally a Saturday (in honour of our Lady) or, if their study schedule made that impossible, a Sunday, and go together to visit a family in the slums of Madrid.

Initially the parish priests of the outlying districts used to give us the addresses of the families they considered were most in need. I remember the parish church of St Christine, at the Extremadura crossroads, near the Casa de Campo, and its parish priest, who would go into a building and blow a whistle to summon everyone from the different apartments so that he could tell them more quickly what he wanted them to know.

There were still parts of the outskirts of Madrid which were in an appalling condition. Many families were still suffering the effects of the Civil War: they were living in shacks built of board and sheets of tin, or in the ruins of bombed or abandoned buildings. Frequently they lacked the basic infrastructure of electricity, running water, and drainage. These people had only the smallest income, not enough to feed themselves adequately or get any warm clothes against the winter cold. On plenty of occasions we found sick people lying alone and uncared for.

All this enabled us to see with our own eyes the utter wretchedness and poverty of so many people. It made a deep impression on us, shaking us out of the irresponsibility and selfishness of comfortable, middle-class boys. When we contrasted this poverty with a student's privileged position, our consciences were quickly moved to feelings of solidarity, and it made us decide to spend much less on ourselves and our amusements. It also helped us pray to God to remedy such evils, when we realised how utterly helpless we were to do anything about them.

Obviously our visits to poor people could not aim to provide a global solution to those appalling conditions. All we could do was practise brotherly Christian charity towards a very small number of people, and bring them some of the warmth of the faith, and a little encouragement, so that they did not feel quite so marginalized. But we thought seriously about being able to do something beneficial for society in the future, when we began to work.

When we were on the way back from these visits and started talking over what we had seen, it was an especially good time for reflecting and making resolutions to improve the way we were living our Christian faith. On more than one occasion the person who had come with me changed his behaviour quite radically and underwent a deep conversion, with lasting effects. I could relate some particular cases, but this is not the right place for it. It will easily be understood that these visits to the poor did as much good to us as to the people we visited.

Catechism classes

We also used to go and help give catechism classes in the parishes of the outlying slum areas, alternating these with our visits to the poor. I say alternating, because we did not usually do both things at the same time, so as not to take too much time away from studying, since transport was so bad in those years that each of the two activities took up a half-day every week. Naturally, we applied to the parish priests for this too, and they would allot us groups of children to teach. Catechism classes too were very good for us as well as the children, because we could see for ourselves, at first hand, the urgent need to teach the truths of the Christian faith to children from the poorest families, socially, spiritually, and culturally speaking. The priests were grateful to us for our help, especially when the time came to prepare the children for their First Holy Communion.

Sports

That year sports were relegated to a low position. We were still living in times when everything was scarce, as a result of the Spanish Civil War and then the Second World War, which was holding up the country's recovery. Our sports were still restricted to football, rowing on the lake in Retiro Park, and some short outings on foot. Anything else was prohibitively expensive for the average student. A small group of us sometimes used to go and do some rudimentary athletics very early in the morning. We would run to an area in front of Nuevos Ministerios. There, on a playing-field of bare earth with the occasional piece of grass, we used to set up some poles and a cord and do high-jumping and long-jumping, and throw a brick or some such object in place of a proper discus. We would then run back again to have a shower and join in the prayer and Mass at the residence.

The people who were most assiduous at this activity were Félix Iñiguez de Onzoño and Javier Domínguez Marroquín, both from Bilbao, the present writer, and one or two others. Félix would later become an architect. Javier was really good at the hundred-metre sprint; later he was to cut short his course in philosophy and law to take over the family business after his father's premature death.

But you really needed to love it. When we were running home down the Paseo de la Castellana, we not uncommonly found ourselves racing alongside trams; as the custom of jogging had not caught on in those days, the workmen on their way to work in the trams used to joke at us with varying degrees of wit.

There was not yet a sports centre on the university campus. For football games the most popular place was still the "Larralde Ground". Our star player was Carlos Arencibia, who was in a different class from the rest. The people who played most were Jesús Larralde himself, Ignacio Orbegozo, the brothers Emilio and Rafael Amann, the people who did the early-morning athletics, and very few more besides.

Get-togethers

The newly arrived residents found what we termed "get-togethers" quite a novelty. We used to have them straight after lunch and the short visit to the Blessed Sacrament, and again after dinner in the evenings. These get-togethers only lasted a few minutes, but they helped to increase the family spirit, strengthen everyone's friendship, and distract people from their exclusive concentration on their studies. Naturally, we would talk spontaneously about national and international news, and topics of interest in the cultural, religious, and human spheres. Time was always a difficulty: some people had classes first thing in the afternoon; others felt they needed to carry the day's work on into the evenings, especially people who were studying for the Engineering Schools' entrance examinations. In spite of these difficulties, a good number of the residents liked the get-togethers and always came to them, finding them relaxing and a way of getting out of our rather enclosed world.

When we had a day's holiday, naturally, the get-togethers lasted a lot longer. We could talk in much more depth about cultural themes or topics of interest and discuss the progress of national sporting events. We did not talk about politics, out of a delicate respect for individual freedom in such matters and a sort of tacit agreement not to risk re-opening wounds from the recent Civil War. In any case, political activity was very severely restricted in Spain because of the well-known circumstances of the times. We talked quite a lot about the way the Second World War was going, and sometimes people told funny stories or jokes. I remember that Jesús Larralde often got them mixed up (I do not know whether he did it on purpose) or else forgot the punch-line: he used to ruin most of his own jokes, but this made us laugh all the more.

Cultural formation

The practice of prayer, the circles, visits to the

poor, catechism classes, get-togethers, sports, and so on, all aimed to contribute to the spiritual and human development of the residents in Jenner Street. As future professional workers who would presumably play an influential role in society one day, they also needed cultural development, to complement what they were acquiring in their respective faculties or schools. In the Jenner Street residence, accordingly, people were encouraged to read major works of literature, history, art, etc. There was not a proper library in the residence at that time. There was only a small collection of these types of books and a few spiritual books on a bookcase in the Oratory itself.

So we started a project to build up a well-chosen, varied library. We had some book-cases made, in a style that matched the decoration of the sitting-room, and little by little began to put books on them. Some were books donated by the residents, and others were bought with money they gave, while still others came from other sources, such as being donated by embassies or official organisations in response to appeals. Drawing up lists of books to buy was a subject which sometimes occupied the Sunday afternoon get-togethers, and this enabled us to explain the characteristics of books and authors worth reading: this sort of public selection was itself a part of their cultural development.

With the passing of the years I have sometimes reflected on the effective fostering of human and spiritual development which was carried out in Jenner

Residence, stimulated by Blessed Josemaría, at the cost of enormous sacrifice and hard work. Judging from what I heard, mainly from my brother Pedro and Paco Botella, they had experienced the same thing in the original residence in Ferraz Street. And it was to continue, spreading out through time and space to acquire its present dimensions in many countries in all five continents. In these residences an effective apostolate is being done, a silent, self-sacrificing kind. So many former residents recall their years in those residences with deep affection and gratitude. I myself, of course, feel deeply indebted for the training and development I received in Jenner Residence and in Moncloa Hall, which succeeded it.

Early friends in the Arts Faculty

Many of my fellow-students in the foundation course at the Arts Faculty whom I met when I began my university course, went on to become famous in the fields of teaching, research, and literature. Examples include Carlos Seco Serrano, later one of the outstanding figures in studies of contemporary Spanish history; even in those days he was a very hard-working student, who displayed an unusual degree of deliberation in his judgements and wisdom in his behaviour. Other friendly and intelligent fellow-students of mine were Yela Granizo, soon to become a famous promoter of psychology, and Antonio López Gómez, an able geographer, who had studied with me at the Ramiro de Maeztu Institute. Four of them went on with me to study Semitic language: Alberto Pascual Villar, Mercedes Arias, Sergio Castellano, and Fr Darío Cavanelas, a Franciscan. Alberto, a very clever and overwhelmingly friendly man, was combining a degree in Arts with one in Law; from there he went straight into Diplomatic School and became Spanish Consul General in Jerusalem. Mercedes, an intelligent woman, worked as a librarian and archivist. Sergio, a worthy man in every respect, died prematurely but not before he had attained a post as assistant teacher of Arabic. Fr Darío was to become one of the great Arabic specialists, holding the chair for Arabic at the University of Granada; he died a few years ago.

But there were other notable colleagues at the beginning: Rafael Asenjo, a Latin student, who would later join Opus Dei and receive ordination to the priesthood; Fr Bacaicoa, a Capuchin and very gifted, who went on to study classics; and many more besides, good and valued friends of mine, with a brilliant future before them, such as José María Cabezalí, later Professor of Spanish Language and Literature; Jorge Manrique, a poet like his namesake; Angel Cabo Alonso; Dr González Abas, a philosopher; José Caba, who left the Arts Faculty to concentrate on law, and became a judge; Vecilla, Tamayo, and Bullón, who became teachers; and Gregorio Verdú, later the founder and Principal of the Anglo-Spanish School located in the El Viso Colony in Madrid.

From them I learnt many excellent things. They contributed to making the postwar years into a time of joy and hope despite all the material shortages. The friendship between all of us was sincere and good-natured. We Arts Faculty students characteristically talked about everything under the sun, and gave our opinion on every matter, both human and divine, constructing theories on *omni re scibili* (everything knowable). We would turn from commenting on Plato's *Republic* to the progress of the Second World War and its consequences. One day we came to the conclusion that before long the whole of North Africa would go up like a powder-keg and throw off the colonial yoke. One must admit that this was prophetic: we were about two decades in advance of events.

We were not so sure who would win the world war. Those were years in which the forces of the Third Reich appeared to be unstoppable, and at first sight it seemed as if Germany would win despite the entry into the conflict of the United States, which did not look like the giant it was later to prove itself to be. Anyway, the information we had was so complex that we were cautious in our predictions of the outcome. Moreover, Gibraltar was a thorn in the side for Spaniards in those days: for more than one, the idea of getting rid of that thorn was an emotive reason – the term "visceral" was not yet current – for wanting to join the combat on the side of Germany, even though it was Hitler's Germany. But obviously, we had not the slightest inkling of the horrors of the Nazi extermination camps.

On the subject of national politics we were more reserved, not wishing to wound one another; the different circumstances of our families, often on opposite sides in the Civil War, were still too recent, and its consequences still weighed on us in various ways. Among the Arts Faculty students there was a genuine desire for harmony.

Religious topics, of course, entered into our discussions. The atmosphere was a generally religious one. I cannot remember any declared agnostics, and I think we were all completely sincere in our beliefs. Many of us were practising Catholics: perhaps the horrors of the Civil War had made my generation, in general, turn our eyes and our hopes towards transcendent values. As I recall, at least three of those who debated on all this later became priests. Certain writers and politicians have referred to this epoch an one of "National Catholicism". This is not the right place to discuss it, but as far as my fellow-students in the Arts Faculty were concerned, any such label would be completely inappropriate. Perhaps students in that faculty have always been too critical, and perhaps too self-opinionated as well, to accept that sort of government interference in people's consciences.

A curious event

Among my fellow-students was Luis Cencillo, who was later to become a priest and a Professor of

Philosophy. He was one of the most brilliant students, and a friendly and communicative person. One day, when I was there, he made some ill-considered and mistaken remarks about Opus Dei; I cannot now remember what stage we were at in our course. We were in the middle of a group of people, in a break between classes, and there was no time to clarify things. But I made an appointment to meet him so as to sort the matter out when we were not in any hurry. We agreed to meet in the Gambrinus Café, one which students often went to, which was located between Alcalá Street and San Jerónimo Street. Luis did not turn up, and neither did he let me know he was not coming. He avoided me several times when our paths crossed in the Arts Faculty, and there the matter rested.

Some time in the 1970s, when I was living in Pamplona, I made a journey to Madrid. As I was walking along Manuel Silvela Street, I heard a car braking and a voice called, "Casciaro, Casciaro!" I stopped. It was Cencillo, who hastily parked his car and came up to me. Without any kind of preamble he announced, "Look, I really am sorry about standing you up that day in the café."

About thirty years had gone by since then. Luis was a man of honour, and his failure to appear must have continued to weigh on his conscience. After three decades, he was making his apologies. He had cleared up the ideas he had previously had about the Work and treated me as affectionately as when we were first friends. Altogether it was a curious and amusing episode with my old friend. Some time later I invited him to an anthropology seminar for teachers, at the University of Navarre, and he came with great pleasure and instructed us with his philosophical considerations, which were penetrating, interesting, some of them disputable, but all brilliantly explained.

Preparing the first priests in Opus Dei

As far as I am aware, from the beginning of the year 1941-42 Blessed Josemaría concerned himself directly with the preparation of some of his sons for the priesthood. Here too the Founder of Opus Dei had absolute faith, a faith "so solid you could cut it", as I heard him say himself on several occasions. One only has to reflect that, canonically, Opus Dei's options were limited at that stage by the 1917 Code of Canon Law. In 1941 the Work had the approval and blessing of the Bishop of Madrid and many other bishops too, but canonically it was nothing more than a Pious Union. This canonical framework did not allow for the ordination of priests, nor their incardination. For the Father's intentions for the future, and in the light of the Work's need for its own priests, the canonical form of Pious Union was simply inadequate and was certainly very little compared with the splendid theological and pastoral reality of Opus Dei even in those days.

It would fall outside the scope of my purpose even to mention the different steps in Opus Dei's canonical journey up to its definitive approval by the

Holy Father Pius XII in 1950 and being canonically constituted a Personal Prelature of the Church in 1982 by Pope John Paul II in line with the new documents of canon law drawn up following the Second Vatican Council.[1]

The faith and foresight of the Founder of Opus Dei in those years is astonishing. Since "Heaven is pledged to the accomplishment of the Work", as he had written some ten years earlier, sooner or later the canonical horizons had to open up. The Church would end up by accommodating Opus Dei within its canonical provision without modifying the spirit and practice that God wanted it to have. Its canonical path has been a long and laborious one, filled with faith, prayer, and mortification and persevering fortitude on the part of the Founder of Opus Dei.

But let us return to the preparation of the future priests who were needed to fulfil what God wanted. Their classes were held in the Centre of Studies in Diego de León Street. If my memory serves, the little group was made up of Alvaro del Portillo, José María Hernández de Garnica, José Luis Múzquiz, and José Orlandis. José Orlandis interrupted his studies not long afterwards to move to Rome with Salvador Canals, in the middle of the Second World War. Blessed Josemaría obtained the best panel of teachers

---

[1] For full details see A. de Fuenmayor, V. Gómez-Iglesias and J. L. Illanes, *The Canonical Path of Opus Dei. The History and Defense of a Charism*, Princeton, New Jersey and Chicago, Scepter Publishers and Midwest Theological Forum, 1994, 655pp.

to be found in Madrid for them: Fr Silvestre Sancho, O.P., a good theologian and philosopher, who had been rector of St. Thomas Aquinas University in Manila; Fr Benito Celada, O.P., a researcher on the Middle East in ancient times and the Bible; Fr José López Ortiz, O.S.A., Professor of History of Law at the University of Madrid, and later Bishop of Tuy-Vigo; José María Bueno Monreal, whom I have already mentioned; Fr Muñiz, O.P.; Justo Pérez de Urbel, O.S.B.; Fr Severino Alvarez, O.P., an outstanding canon lawyer; Don Máximo Yurramendi, later Bishop of Ciudad Rodrigo; and some others whose names escape me. I remember, as an incident of no importance, that on one occasion Blessed Josemaría gave me, in person, the job of taking an envelope to one of these teachers at his home address, containing his payment for the classes he had taught.

The efforts which the group put into attaining a deep theological training was both intense and exemplary. As a consequence they obtained brilliant results in the examinations of the Madrid Diocesan Seminary. This can be ascertained from the records of the subjects in question, and I was told so myself, years later, by Don Joaquín Blázquez and Don Ramiro López Gallego, both Canons at Madrid Cathedral, teachers of dogmatic theology at the above-mentioned seminary, and members of the Francisco Suárez Theological Institute of the CSIC (*Consejo Superior de Investigaciones Científicas*, or Higher Academic Research Council).

Journey to Torrevieja

I began these pages with my memories of summer 1936 in Torrevieja, and I will finish with my last stay in the town where I spent my childhood and adolescence.

The academic year 1941-42 was over. One day in the Centre at Diego de León Street, probably at the beginning of July 1942, Blessed Josemaría told me that he thought I should go to Torrevieja for a few days to see my family and, in his words, "to soak yourself a bit in the sea, which will do you a lot of good and will mean you can rest after the heat of Madrid."

My parents were still in Oran, and my grandfather, Julio Casciaro, had died on 1 January 1942. The only people in Torrevieja were his widow, my grandmother Soledad, and a good number of uncles, aunts, and cousins, who were spending their summer holidays at Los Hoyos as usual. Everyone was delighted, especially my grandmother, because they had not seen me for a long time. My stay in Torrevieja with my relations showed me Blessed Josemaría's affection and concern for myself and my family, because neither I nor my brother had said a word to him about it; the idea came from the Father himself.

The journey brought some indirect benefits as well. For one thing, Monsieur and Madame Martin, the childless French couple, both teachers at the French Lycée in Oran, who had generously welcomed my parents into their home, decided to stop off for a few days in Torrevieja on their way to France for their holidays, to meet their guests' family. They were thus able to see for themselves that they belonged to a highly respected family. They stayed at Los Hoyos for several days, at the same time as I was there. Naturally, out of our real gratitude, my grandmother and I lavished attention and affection on them. My grandmother gave them her own bedroom, which was the best in the house.

The Martins were in their forties and so were able to take part in some water-sports such as canoeing in the harbour and in the open sea, which was usually calm in summer. When they got back to Oran, my parents told us in their letters how very happy they were to have met the family and to have been taken such good care of. They had always treated my parents extremely well, and from that time on this became still more pronounced. Until my parents returned to Spain in 1947 the Martins would not consent to their moving out of their house. As on previous occasions, God's providence had inspired Blessed Josemaría with ideas which resulted in spiritual favours and human consolations for my parents.

Besides all this, I met Uncle Diego and his family, who had gone to Torrevieja for the summer. Spending those few days together meant a lot to them and to me. They perfectly understood my decision to stay in Madrid and were very interested to hear about my studies. Uncle Diego and I talked endlessly about everything in this world and beyond it. We swam till we were exhausted, and some afternoons, after a protracted lunch-table conversation, we studied German together, since we were both at more or less the same level.

When I got back from Torrevieja Blessed Josemaría called me to talk to him for a while. He asked after everything that had happened and gave me an affectionate scolding for having written to them very little during my stay in Torrevieja, just like a good father and a good mother whose son has been away for a few weeks and who have not had all the frequent news of him their hearts desire.

Here I bring my account to a conventional close. I think I have achieved what I set out to do. I have evoked those three first years, from May 1939 to August 1942, when in one way or another I was close to the Founder of Opus Dei and also close to Grandmother and Aunt Carmen, and that set of men who, before me or at the same time as me, had great faith in God and in Blessed Josemaría and have since remained faithful to what God asked of them. Words cannot express all that this living history, which began then and still continues, means to my soul.

Epilogue

I was intending to write a short account. On reaching the end I think one conclusion is obvious: with Blessed Josemaría one felt, that is we all felt, loved and impelled to love. He was a man who, above all, knew how to love. "Passionately Loving the World" is the title of one of his most significant homilies, given in Pamplona on 8 October 1967, on the Navarre University Campus before a crowd of 20-30,000 people. I was lucky enough to be there on that occasion. Perhaps that homily can be taken as a compendium of his whole spiritual and human message.

Love for God and other people was a gift which God gave the Founder of Opus Dei, who responded to it with exceptional generosity. He learnt that love in the fire of his persevering prayer and his "silent, hidden sacrifice", together with his ever-renewed commitment to fulfilling God's Will. The reason for this is that God our Father is Love: a Love that leads him to give his own Only-begotten Son.[1] A Love,

---

[1] John 3:16-17.

common to each of the Divine Persons, which is the deepest reason why the Eternal Word became man and lived among men, why the Holy Spirit has been sent to the Church and to each of the faithful.

Dear reader: you and I, disciples of Jesus, can follow no other path than the one which Jesus Christ, God and Man, marked out and travelled along himself, followed by all the saints, whatever their individual messages may have been. But I would not want to finish by giving a spiritual talk. We have paused to consider one of them, a contemporary of our own, Blessed Josemaría, and only in some aspects of his life over a very few years, as seen by a young and inexpert witness.

On calling to mind the episodes I have related, I feel deeply grateful to Blessed Josemaría because the whole of his life was a living and arresting lesson. After him my gratitude goes out to all those men whose way of acting was a pointer for me of how to be good and behave well. I have spoken of them in the course of writing about these simple, family-like episodes and events. Most of the older ones have now died, especially over these last few years, as can be seen from the short biographical notes. They co-operated unreservedly with the Founder in order, as he said, "to do Opus Dei on earth by being Opus Dei yourself." In these men, of whom some have now been faithful right up to their deaths and others are still fighting in this life, I saw, and still see, the perfect expression of our Lord Jesus Christ's words,

"Let your light so shine before men that they may see your good works and give glory to your Father who is in heaven."[2]

The different episodes happened quite naturally and prosaically. But on the inside there was a spirit not perceptible to the senses, which was nevertheless the basic reason for everything that happened. This spirit was and still is like the soul, which cannot be seen but which is what gives life to and is expressed through the body. Or, if you prefer, like the salt which disappears but gives flavour to the food: "the salt of the world".[3]

My experience started in 1939, when, at the end of the Spanish Civil War, a time of truly providential expansion and growth began for the Work. The Opus Dei that I met was a small family with spiritual ties, a handful of young men. Only the Founder, Isidoro Zorzano, and José María Albareda were around forty; most of them were between twenty and thirty. They were students or had just started work in the intellectual professions. Now there are many thousands of women and men in the Work. There are still professional people and graduates from universities and other places of higher education; but many more work in non-intellectual jobs, such as miners, factory workers, agricultural workers, domestic employees, nurses, office-workers in private companies and in public organizations, taxi-drivers, security guards,

---

[2] Matt 5:16.
[3] Cf. Matt 5:13.

small businessmen, and traders... At that time there was only one priest, the Founder. Now there are more than 1,500 priests incardinated into the Prelature of Opus Dei and still more diocesan priests incardinated into their own dioceses, who live by the spirit of Opus Dei personally, in the faithful fulfilment of the tasks they are given by their respective bishops. Both lay-people and clergy, women and men, knowing themselves to be "a tiny part of the Church", as Blessed Josemaría defined Opus Dei on occasions, dedicate their whole existence, amidst their daily work and their family and social duties, to spreading the Christian faith and serving their equals, other men and women throughout a large part of the world.

Opus Dei's circumstances and its canonical form have changed. But the life of the few people whom I have described mainly through stories and incidents and the life of the thousands mentioned above, whether young or old, is identical: their spirit and their piety, their apostolic zeal and the forms their apostolate takes, their desire to surpass themselves individually in their ordinary duties, and their quest for Christian holiness wherever God has placed them in this world are all just the same. Nor has there been any change in the sincere, trusting sense of being children to the Father and Prelate of Opus Dei, which we first felt in relation to our holy Founder and which now continues to be lived with the same characteristics towards his successors, first Monsignor Alvaro del Portillo and now, since his death in 1994,

Monsignor Javier Echevarría. I cannot fail to see God's loving Providence in all this.

To sum up, I find that the life of the men and women of Opus Dei is the same now as it was more than half a century ago. The Prelature of Opus Dei is still a family, whose spiritual ties are just as strong. Although it is now a very numerous family taken as a whole, it is still a small one in each single centre, where people's lives are characterized by the same fraternity and homely warmth. This is how God wants it to be, and this lifestyle has been handed on like the baton in a relay-race.

The vocational call to Opus Dei is a grace given by God alone. But, as with so many things in the natural and supernatural spheres, the ground first needs to be well fertilized and then cultivated: I met both aspects from the start, and I still find them today in the faithful of the Prelature wherever I go. The first person in Opus Dei whom I met along the way was my own brother, Pedro. I would just like to add two paragraphs from the letter which the Bishop Prelate of Opus Dei, Monsignor Javier Echevarría, wrote to me on 24 March 1995, the day after Pedro's death, because it underlines some constants in the faithful of the Prelature: affection, loyalty, the sense of filiation to the Father and Prelate of the Work, and fraternity.

"Dearest Pepe,

May Jesus look after you for me! With my heart filled with sorrow I am writing you these lines to share in your pain over the death of our much-loved

Pedro (may he rest in peace). Although we knew that he might leave us at any moment, it is very hard to part from someone who was such a faithful son to our Founder: how much I have prayed for him to get better over these past months! But the Lord has disposed things so that now he can help us from Heaven, with his effective intercession, after setting us a magnificent example of dedication, including during his illness, which he endured with the style and the supernatural outlook which were always his.

... José María, I am praying for you very specially right now, that you too may be as loyal as your brother was for sixty years. Pray frequently through Pedro's intercession, and commit my intentions to him.

... Having a great desire to see you, I bless you with immense affection,

Your Father

+ Javier."

Something else that made an impact from the very first time I met Blessed Josemaría was his spirit of freedom. How often I heard him say, about all sorts of circumstances, "Long live freedom!" Right from the start, our Father educated us – some of us could almost say he brought us up – "in freedom". I have recalled some episodes concerning this. I want to underline the feeling that we have always had in Opus Dei of being at home, as any member of a Christian family feels when with his or her family, and of knowing that we are personally responsible for the whole family's success. This gives us maturity, freedom, and responsibility from our earliest years in the Work.

Finally, at various places in the central buildings of the Prelature in Rome, we read the inscription *Vale la pena*, "it is worth while", a motto we often heard the Founder of the Work use, which expresses the value of giving ourselves to God, and directs us towards eternal blessedness.

Indeed, when one looks back on those first years of God's call, and then takes a look at the years that followed, one feels the truth of these words very deeply. It was worth while following Blessed Josemaría because that meant, and means, going hand-in-hand with him to our Lord Jesus Christ. It is an adventure but also a safe "path" through the earth to heaven. After more than half a century, how joyful and consoling it is, amidst all my personal failings, to have followed the route God showed me in my early youth! It is true that the writer of these recollections was carried along for many years without making very much effort for his own part: perhaps the only thing I did was to put my faith in God and trust in Blessed Josemaría, who was the instrument God used to guide us to the end, in the bosom of our Holy Mother the Church.

I thank God, One and Three, in the depths of my being, for the divine call he made me discover in my earliest years, and because he has kept me firm in my first decision. I have been sustained ever more strongly, day after day, by a joyful ambition to contribute with other people to the marvellous adventure of "doing Opus Dei on earth". On looking back, it is indeed clear that it was worth while making that journey. Yes, once and a thousand times, it was worth while, it is worth while.

Laus Deo Virginique Matri.